"Inspiring, enchanting, yet completely accessible . . . living outside has never felt so within reach. Frankly, even if you don't have an inch of outdoor space, you'll still be totally transported."

—Joanna Saltz, editorial director of *House Beautiful*

"Finally, garden and design come together seamlessly in this gorgeous, more-than-a-gardening book where authors Isa and Jenny enthusiastically walk us through dozens of outdoor rooms and teach us how to masterfully create our very own stylish retreat no matter how big or small our space."

—Steele Marcoux, editor in chief of *Veranda*

"Gardens can be the most magical part of any home and this luscious new book absolutely inspired me to get right out into my own garden and fix it up. The photos and all the lovely ideas within them are so accessible and delicious you won't put this book down."

—Maxwell Ryan, founder of Apartment Therapy

Isa Hendry Eaton &
Jennifer Blaise Kramer

SMALL GARDEN STYLE

A Design Guide for Outdoor Rooms and Containers

Photography by
Leela Cyd

TEN SPEED PRESS
California | New York

contents

Introduction 1

1 FIND YOUR SMALL GARDEN STYLE 7

2 SMALL GARDEN DESIGN SCHOOL 63

3 SMALL GARDEN FLOORS, WALLS,
AND CEILINGS 87

4 TOP-TO-BOTTOM PLANT SELECTION 105

5 CONTAINER GARDENS 127

6 DESIGNER TOOL KIT 159

Landscape Lingo 172

Top Plant Picks 174

Thank Yous! 178

Contributors 180

Index 182

Introduction

Small gardens are enchanting. It's no accident that Frances Hodgson Burnett's captivating childhood classic, *The Secret Garden*, told a story of transformation against the backdrop of a little garden that could. With heart and hard work, children nurtured this neglected space until everyone and everything inside the enclosed walls became the best version of themselves. That's the promise of a garden—a joyful place where we can use the power of the outdoors to refuel and reconnect with our friends and family. With a little thought and planning, small spaces in particular can serve as the most livable and lovely garden rooms that truly expand our living space and fulfill that promise of beauty, joy, and connection.

Whatever your space—an urban balcony, a postage stamp patio, or a suburban backyard—this book will help you define and refine your bit of earth. Maybe you're looking for a full garden makeover or you simply want to fluff the porch with new pots that complement your house and reflect your indoor style; we've got your back. Containers are a great way to try out new garden tricks before moving onto larger spaces. They can also play a starring role in a well-designed small garden. They can add architectural interest (without hiring an architect), soften a space to make it feel like a warm hug after work, or define a confusing entry so your guests stop wandering in through the side gate. Containers accomplish all of this and have the flexibility to move with you if you move on.

However small in square footage, your garden can be as brilliant and transporting as possible, and we will get you there. Like any project, the magic is achieved with a little thought and planning before stepping foot in a garden shop. Heading to the nursery without a plan is like going to the grocery store hungry. You might buy heaps of beautiful ingredients, but you can't cook a balanced a meal when you get home, let alone impress your dinner guests. Just as a beloved cookbook is a reassuring guide for the kitchen, we hope this book will become your garden confidant, your source for continued

inspiration translated into real recipes with professional tips and tricks to streamline the shopping and spruce up the garden, while giving answers along the way to those inevitable questions.

When we first brainstormed this book, recipes were front and center. Much like you'd build out your dinner from scratch, we wanted to start with a small, manageable space—or even the smallest garden planter—and provide a step-by-step guide full of how-to tips, winning combinations, and the design thinking behind why certain plants work together. We also wanted to pull style into the conversation to connect your personal point of view and secret lifestyle aspirations (how you dream to live!) to your own outdoor space. *Small Garden Style* is all of that, sharing our best secrets and plant recipes along with other easy, accessible ideas for a range of small garden styles.

Some of you might be seasoned pros looking for insider secrets— you've come to the right place! Or you might be a garden novice reading these pages with trepidation—no worries, you have nothing to fear! Because guess what—we are all of you. Your two authors, Isa and Jenny, are friends, writers, fellow moms of three each, and nearly neighbors, living a mile apart in Santa Barbara. We have lived in the Northeast, Midwest, and Northwest before landing permanently in California. We understand first-hand what it means to garden small—from potted herbs on the San Francisco fire escape, to seasonal shrubs on a Minneapolis front porch, to winterized boxwoods on a Boston brick patio, to our own Santa Barbara gardens with a bit more sunshine. Even the professional Isa Bird Landscape Design projects that cover several acres still require smaller, defined, outdoor rooms to make the gardens comfortable for living.

One of us is seasoned and one of us is a newcomer, and together we keep it real and keep it fun. Isa, the pro, launched Isa Bird Landscape Design as a natural extension of her graphic design and letterpress business, combining her deep knowledge of plants with a career understanding of visual communication that

"We wanted to start with a small, manageable space—or even the smallest garden planter—and provide a step-by-step guide full of how-to tips and winning combinations."

makes her real-life designs graphic, layered, and lush whether big or small. Isa's gardens have also been photographed for *Better Homes and Gardens, HGTV Magazine, Garden Design* magazine, and *Santa Barbara Magazine*. Jenny, the enthusiastic rookie gardener, is a design writer who has spent two decades covering homes and gardens across the country for publications including *Better Homes and Gardens, Condé Nast Traveler, Domino, House Beautiful*, and *Sunset*. She can reupholster living room chairs in vintage fabric or confidently match tile and wallpaper, yet the garden store to garden bed crisis was real. Learning the ropes from a pro came with a lot of laughs, coffees, and croissants in Jenny's secret olive garden, and homegrown salads and fizzy drinks on Isa's treehouse deck (sensing a food theme here?). Under the blue sky, we talked about how to relay the best garden advice to others in a fresh way that feels like those favorite cookbooks and design books, not like a plant encyclopedia. Our common goal? How to break it down without having a breakdown.

Together, we hope this book helps you think about your small garden as another room of your home. Just like the interiors, the outdoor space should be defined with garden "floors" covered with gravel, gorgeous ground cover, or creeping herbs and "walls" made of a leafy hedge or a striking row of potted trees. In this book you'll find easy ways to get started right away on everything from the design process (yes, you can plan and spray paint a pathway like a pro) to getting your hands dirty arranging striking plant groupings. Trust us, you'll never wind up in a nursery nightmare again with this strategy. We have weekend projects from vertical gardens to instant orchards, front-door wreaths to easy water features. Call your guests: you'll be throwing that magazine-style garden party before you know it. Small gardens, big style, that's our promise. Loving and living in your garden—just like your other favorite rooms inside—is what it's all about. Let's roll up our sleeves and get started; we're here for you.

XO

Isa + Jenny

FIND YOUR SMALL GARDEN STYLE

Your garden, like everything else in your life, should reflect your individual style. This is essential in the small garden to help your space feel larger, not smaller. When working in a limited space, those misaligned extras—elements that stray from your style—can stick out like a sore thumb. A strong point of view keeps you from overfilling and cluttering up tight spaces and helps you create a cohesive look and calm oasis. Nailing your style will help you make easier, faster decisions when you're designing your garden. And so, we start the style journey with a personal look at who will enjoy your garden, how you want to live in your space, the mood you want to create, and the feeling that will call you outdoors over and over again. To help define your style, our quiz in the pages ahead is all about you—what you like, what you drink, and what movies make you tick. Are you wondering why water versus wine or your favorite reading chair has anything to do with garden design? Good question. Style translates from our closet to our living room to our garden and ensures a garden functions well for your lifestyle.

Elevator Pitch for Your Garden

A fun way to visualize the style, mood, and purpose of your garden is to write its elevator pitch in twenty-five words or less. Here we share our not-so-secret garden dreams.

Jenny: My European-style courtyard with romantic vines and olive trees is a transporting, social space for intimate dinner parties and lively, late-night conversation with friends.

Isa: My woodsy, peaceful oasis with breezy grasses and modern plantings under the oaks has inviting spaces for family brunches and for cozy evenings by the fire.

Function (Who, What, When)

This is *your* garden and it should work comfortably for the way you live. It's important to take a look at your lifestyle, your tribe, and how you want to spend time with *or* without them (we're not judging!) before you start designing or go plant shopping. Start with these questions to help decide what to include in your garden and why. Then you can get real about your space, time, and budget constraints.

- What would you like to *do* in your garden? Host dinner parties and family gatherings, unwind, toss squeaky toys for your Doodle and toddler, enjoy your morning coffee?

- What outdoor "room" do you hope to include? A kitchen for cooking and grilling, dining room, living room, breakfast room, family rumpus room, nap room?

- What time of day will you spend the most time outdoors? Where is the sun at this time? Do you need shade or warmth?

- Who will use your garden? Kids, pets, friends, neighbors? If you have kids or pets, can they be free-range or do they need a contained area? Bee or plant allergies?

- How many people will use your space and how often? Will you have big family gatherings or intimate groups or do you want flexibility for both?

Style + Mood

Consider your home's architectural style and your personal decor style when planning your garden to seamlessly merge form and function. Start a mood board and make a collage of your ideas using Pinterest, Houzz, iPhone snaps, garden books like this one, and magazine clippings. Don't forget to include items you already own and love. Pay special attention to that same photo you find yourself pinning or gazing at over and over again (Just like a spirit animal representing your inner self and style, this may be your spirit garden!). Ask yourself the following questions to hone in on style and feeling.

- How do you want your garden to feel? Peaceful, vibrant, interesting, stunning, clean, eclectic, cool, warm, full, open?

- What is the style of your home? Some homes are more "neutral" than others and can pair with a range of gardens. Homes with a strong historical or architectural style will strongly dictate how the landscape should look.

- Are there any plants, trees, or colors that you must (or must not!) have?

- What is the setting and location of your home? Promise us that you will not create a beach-themed garden on your suburban Ohio deck or build a rustic log gazebo in the backyard of your California beach bungalow.

Style Quiz

Take this find-your-style quiz (no studying required!), and you'll be surprised how much your lifestyle can, and should, influence your outdoor space. It's okay to circle more than one answer since most people have a primary and secondary style that can work together. After you get your results, take a tour through *all* eight garden styles showcased in this chapter. Chances are that your personal style will draw elements from more than one of our featured gardens.

1. **You start your morning routine with:**
   A. Black coffee and a cold shower.
   B. A mug of dark roast while listening to a podcast and checking email.
   C. Sipping homemade kale and ginger green juice over your daily gratitude journal.
   D. A few sun salutations before collecting fresh eggs from the coop.
   E. Sitting with a cup of jasmine green tea for quiet, loving-kindness meditation.
   F. A glass of tangerine juice and half a ruby grapefruit from the turquoise bowl on the kitchen counter.
   G. French press coffee and a croissant over the daily newspaper.
   H. A pot of Earl Grey tea, the morning news, and hustling the kids to the school bus.

2. **Your favorite place to relax in at home is:**
   A. A vintage white Bertoia chair, structured and stylish.
   B. A black leather Eames lounge chair, hands down.
   C. A woven hammock to curl up in and gaze at the trees.
   D. A handmade chair covered in sheepskins.
   E. A carved daybed to lie down and quiet the mind.
   F. A neon Acapulco chair outside in the sun.
   G. A pair of Fermob bistro chairs while catching up with an old friend.
   H. An old wicker armchair that looks great indoors or out, layered with quilts.

3. **Your ideal mode of transportation is:**
   A. A Tesla, charged and ready in the garage.
   B. A vintage Land Cruiser.
   C. Hiking shoes, heading for the mountains.
   D. Public transportation ideally, or an electric bike when that's not an option.
   E. Barefoot and dancing or a camper, ready for the next music festival.
   F. A bright yellow beach cruiser coasting with friends into a watercolor sunset.
   G. A Vespa, a basket, and a dream!
   H. A Jeep Wagoneer with wood paneling, perfect for bringing home a Christmas tree!

4. **Books we might find on your nightstand are:**
   A. Books sound like clutter. You must be thinking of a tablet.
   B. The latest cookbook signed by the chef.
   C. *The Happiness Project* by Gretchen Rubin.
   D. *The Art of Fermentation* by Sandor Ellix Katz.
   E. *The Alchemist* by Paulo Coelho or anything by Deepak Chopra.

F. *Styling for Instagram* by Leela Cyd and a few books by Dr. Seuss.

G. Hemingway's *The Sun Also Rises* or anything by John Steinbeck.

H. *Pride and Prejudice* and/or anything by Martha Stewart.

5. **The accessories that live on your couch are:**

A. Nothing! Why hide the lines of a custom chaise?

B. Geometric black and white pillows.

C. A soft, cream-colored alpaca throw.

D. An heirloom quilt my grandmother made in a sewing circle.

E. Indigo dip-dyed lumbar pillows.

F. A mishmash of throw pillows in bright shades and shapes.

G. Sun-faded fabrics found at the markets on a trip to Europe.

H. Ticking stripes to play up the Buffalo check upholstery.

6. **The movie that best describes your dream garden is:**

A. *The Great Gatsby*: manicured and pristine.

B. *The Kids Are Alright*: urban and culinary.

C. *The Secret Garden*: tended with love.

D. *Gone with the Wind*: rural and hardworking.

E. *Eat, Pray, Love*: wild and exotic.

F. *The Lorax*: fun and colorful.

G. *The Godfather*: sunny and dreamy.

H. *It's Complicated*: organized and beautiful.

7. **An outdoor party at home usually looks like this:**

A. Lounge music pumping from the speakers, with cocktails and sushi making the rounds.

B. Tacos, tequila, good music, and friends.

C. Wine and salad with edible flowers from the garden for book club.

D. Farm-to-table ranch-style dinner, grilling local meats and infusing craft cocktails.

E. Take-out Indian with a few close friends sitting on poufs with candles and guitars.

F. A birthday party for the kids with colorful streamers, cake, and lots of running around.

G. A long table for a family-style Italian dinner with red wine flowing and Dean Martin playing.

H. Neighborhood barbecue with all generations, homemade ice cream, and horseshoes.

8. **If your style turned into a tree, the tree would be:**

A. A fence post cactus. A twist on a tall potted tree, but way cooler and less messy.

B. A dwarf orange or kumquat tree— great for garnishes.

C. A shady old oak, inviting and rooted.

D. An apple tree that's pretty and prolific.

E. A silver Mexican palm tree, exotic and alluring.

F. A pomegranate tree bursting with fruit.

G. A heritage olive tree that looks like it's been there forever.

H. A magnolia, stunning at every season.

9. **Your dream vacation is:**

   A. A ski trip to the Alps.

   B. Copenhagen for design and shopping.

   C. An eco-lodge in Nicaragua, hiking and exploring.

   D. A culinary weekend at Blue Stone Farms in Upstate New York.

   E. A soul-searching trek to Nepal.

   F. A Hawaiian Island adventure full of flowering leis and pineapple punch.

   G. Sailing the ancient Greek Islands.

   H. Summer in Kennebunkport, Maine, with lobster rolls and beach reads.

10. **Happy hour comes and you reach for:**

   A. Vodka, neat, in a rimless glass.

   B. Mezcal from a walking tour in Oaxaca.

   C. Crisp, organic Chardonnay.

   D. A refreshing glass of home brew kombucha.

   E. A warm cup of maté tea.

   F. A cranberry fizz with a slice of lime.

   G. A large, long-stem glass of Chateauneuf-du-Pape.

   H. Homemade lemonade with the kids—then an Old-Fashioned after they're in bed!

Tally your answers and find your small garden style (and it's OK to have a couple that work together)!

| A | If you were mostly As, turn to CLEAN MINIMALIST, page 40. |

| B | If you were mostly Bs, turn to BOLD ECLECTIC, page 24. |

| C | If you were mostly Cs, turn to ORGANIC MODERN, page 18. |

| D | If you were mostly Ds, turn to URBAN HOMESTEAD, page 30. |

| E | If you were mostly Es, turn to GLOBAL BOHO, page 44. |

| F | If you were mostly Fs, turn to COLOR PLAY, page 50. |

| G | If you were mostly Gs, turn to OLD WORLD, page 54. |

| H | If you were mostly Hs, turn to NEW TRADITIONAL, page 34. |

"Think about your small garden as another room of your home."

Organic Modern

By day you steal a moment in the breezy, woven hammock to take in the fresh air; by nightfall, it's all about friends by the fire, with plenty of cozy blankets nearby. But your modern sensibilities keep your organic style and textures more naturally crisp than crunchy. Give your garden that same heartwarming touch that you bring to your dinner parties with earthy details designed in modern lines. Just a careful balance of the right elements—fire, water, flora—and a healthy mix of lines and curves. Your fresh style, from that perfect flowing dress to garden-to-table cocktails, will translate just as well outside.

CIRCLE OF LIFE

A circle symbolizes unity, eternity, togetherness, and all those things you probably love. Build your gathering place in the garden around a circle. No matter how wide or narrow your outdoor space, surround it with a lush planted border.

CAMPFIRE

Nothing brings people together more than a warm fire. Build your circle around a fire pit—store-bought, custom, or repurposed—such as this gas fire bowl created from a concrete container.

PLANT ROOTS

If you're lucky enough to have inherited an old tree, then soak up those late afternoon rays. If not, plant a couple of new trees to anchor your space; pearl acacia (*Acacia podalyriifolia*) is shown here. The high-low contrast will add an earthy connection.

Get the Look

- Mixed ornamental grasses
- Textured shrubs and small patio trees
- Flagstone and rustic stone planters
- Natural boulders buried in planter beds
- Round fire pit (the campfire!)
- Circle of chairs, textured pillows, and throws

PLANT RECIPE: ORGANIC MODERN GARDEN ▶

Trees: *Acacia podalyriifolia*, *Quercus agrifolia*. Grasses: *Sesleria autumnalis*, *Sesleria caerulea*, *Chondropetalum tectorum*, *Festuca glauca* 'Elijah Blue'. **Shrub:** *Leucadendron* 'Winter Red'. Succulents: *Cotyledon orbiculata*, *Echeveria imbricata*, *Aeonium canariense*, *Echeveria* 'Cante', *Echeveria elegans*, *Echeveria agavoides* 'Ebony', *Graptopetalum paraguayense*.

ORGANIC S'MORES GARDEN

A fire element in the garden draws people together around the literal, irresistible campfire. Outdoor fire pits and fireplaces add warmth to allow your parties to stay outside longer into the evening and stretch out the season. They are natural magnets for conversation, cocktail parties, and s'mores—make sure to grow fresh mint for a surprise layer. Wood-burning chimineas and propane fire pits can be found at most hardware stores, but we like to repurpose concrete containers into custom fire features that look high-end but are lighter on the budget.

CONVERT A REGULAR POT INTO A FAB FIRE PIT

1. Consult with local codes and permit requirements and hire a licensed plumber for gas work! Or, use a portable propane tank and conceal it with a tank cover that can double as a side table.

2. Select a concrete container for size and shape to work with your style—round reads organic and casual while rectangles skew modern and formal.

3. Drill two holes in the bottom for drainage, plus one hole for the gas line in the bottom center of the container, and one hole for the key valve in the side, 4 inches below the rim.

4. Place your fire pit in the desired location with the gas line stub through the bottom center and the key valve hole facing away from view. Select a stainless steel fire ring that is at least 12 inches smaller in diameter than the container. The ring should sit 4 inches below the rim of the container. The exterior metal key valve is inserted through the hole in the side of the planter, level with the interior fire ring.

5. Fill the entire container with high-heat-rated lava rocks or fire balls until the fire ring is covered with 2 inches of rocks.

6. Add a metal or wood lid for the fire pit to double as a coffee table when *not* in use.

Bold Eclectic

More is more! Go big or go home! You're not afraid of making a statement and every part of your life agrees. You're often the life of the party—and the host—and naturally your home and garden should also be big and bold. Eclectic design means not having to choose—a little bit modern, a little bit vintage. It allows for patterns, textures, and shapes to cohabitate in one space so you can layer in your favorite plants and textiles of the moment. It's about living large in the small garden.

GEO GRAPHICS

Wherever you live, whatever the size, an outdoor patio can be completely transformed into a contained gathering space. If you have the benefit of planning the space from the start, consider adding graphic geometric hardscape, such as bold cement tile or brick in a chevron pattern, to give the room energy and movement.

GARDEN UP

Enlist the walls as unused space for your potted plants to explore. Train plants and vines to climb up, letting the vibrant shapes and leaf forms pop against white walls and act as a living wallpaper that is one hundred percent original—just like you.

AMP UP THE LIGHTING

It may sound counterintuitive, but oversized lighting can work wonders in a small outdoor space. An elegant iron chandelier or deep, dark drum shade gives a glow overhead and will make people want to linger longer.

PLANT RECIPE: BOLD ECLECTIC GARDEN ▶

Containers: *Ficus triangularis, Polystichum munitum, Maranta leuconeura, Rhipsalis baccifera, Howea forsteriana, Senecio radicans.*

Get the Look

- Light, dark, and lime-green plants with plenty of texture
- Vines growing up, plants spilling down
- Wall planters on white walls

- Geometric tabletop planters
- Bold, black-and-white cement tile
- Oversized statement lights and linear cafe chairs

COOL RESTAURANT STYLE AT HOME

We love when a hot, new bar or eatery opens in town, and everyone's buzzing and posting about the look. The tables! The tile! The glasses! Often what helps make a hip, urban restaurant feel fresh and alive is actually the plants. They add as much electricity as those must-have overhead pendants. Tight patios, open-air or covered, are the perfect small garden spaces to get that restaurant style at home—and if they're located off the kitchen, even better.

This scene may look fancy shmancy, but a cold-water bartender's prep sink is basically a glorified garden hose. (Check your local codes, but such sinks can often drain into a simple gravel pit). Raise the wet bar with a few indoor decor elements like mirrors and tea towels, then layer in a heap of plants that'll leave the room shaken *and* stirred.

GET THE ROCK STAR BAR LOOK

1. Pick a sophisticated color palette like this one in shades of gray and metallic.

2. Hang a large mirror on the wall to bounce light around a small space.

3. Choose containers with three different shapes and heights. Stick to a tight color palette (grays) and sophisticated finish (matte and metallic) to keep the look cohesive.

4. Use cake stands to elevate small containers.

5. Choose plants with compelling foliage shapes, textures, colors, and forms. (Blooms and youth are fleeting, but character lasts forever!)

6. Leave room for the glasses!

The Bold Bartender

A Variegated rubber plant (*Ficus elastica* 'Variegata')

B Chinese money plant (*Pilea peperomioides*)

C Asparagus fern (*Asparagus densiflorus* 'Myers')

D Wax plant (*Hoya carnosa*)

E String of hearts (*Ceropegia woodii*)

Urban Homestead

You dream of wide open spaces and life like it used to be. But you live in the modern world without vast acreage and can hear the city bus pass out front. Don't give up those homesteading dreams too quickly. Small city homes can still bring in hip heritage elements of growing, fermenting, beekeeping, and farming. You might have to share the outdoor dining room with the chickens, but a mini farm adds charm and comes with built-in entertainment. Dress up your coop and transform it into a garden focal point. To keep the homestead from getting lost down a country road, fluff your nest with hip planters and trendy accessories.

SPACE + SCALE

Measure carefully and work your backyard space by using every square foot with livable, plantable, and farmable areas. Tall planted walls take up little floor space by relying on vines and bamboo. Bench seating can squeeze eight at this petite table and the two-story chicken coop gives the girls space without dominating the garden.

FREE RANGE

Animals will eat almost anything they can reach—especially juicy succulents, some of which may be poisonous. For free-range birds, choose nontoxic, low-level plants such as grasses, herbs, rosemary, and lavender. For those plants you can't stand to see pecked, we suggest cute expandable willow fencing available at most garden stores.

Get the Look

- Edible herbs
- Low ornamental grasses
- Gold gravel
- Faux sheepskin
- Chicken coop—custom or store-bought
- Modern metal farm table with wire chairs

PLANT RECIPE: URBAN HOMESTEAD GARDEN ▶

Screening: *Bambusa oldhamii, Hedera helix.* (Both timber bamboo and English ivy are potentially dominating plants and can spread like crazy! Use containers to keep them under control in the small garden.) **Herbs:** *Origanum vulgare* subsp. *hirtum, Origanum vulgare* 'Aureum', *Thymus vulgaris, Teucrium chamaedrys.* **Grass:** *Carex divulsa.* **Shrubs:** *Olea europaea* 'Montra', *Coprosma repens* 'Marble Queen'.

SPICE UP THE BACKYARD

Hang mid-century staghorn ferns on the coop and get fresh with paint for those morning eggs. Fill a wine barrel with recipe-ready red hot chile peppers. Caution—these chocolate habanero and black cobra chiles are as hot as they look! Set a centerpiece with two colors of oregano (golden and Greek) for a high-contrast look in a geometric container.

New Traditional

Summer on the Cape. Winter at the cabin. Lemonade on the porch. You're all about tradition just like your grandparents, but your style is unequivocally yours. New traditionalists are both big-hearted and rule-breakers. You might be the one to gather the family now at Thanksgiving but you made all the succulent centerpieces, stitched the napkins from vintage tea towels, and you'll probably be leading the dance-off before dessert. Take your boldness outside and mix up plants and flowers just like you play with patterns and prints.

GRANNY CHIC

Familiar focal points with a twist are a must for new traditional style. Think English ivy, boxwood topiaries, or climbing purple morning glories—just like you remember from years back but with variations of species, shapes, or containers. Take grandma's favorite blooms and plant them in modern pots, throw a cactus in the pedestal urn, and call the shots in your own stylish way.

PERFECT PATINA

Durable materials are quick studies for this style. If you have the opportunity to layer in cobblestone or bluestone, you're off to a running start. If not, add stone planters and galvanized metal tubs for a quick fix—the hardware store sells them, and they make great, affordable, new traditional containers.

A TWIST ON TRADITION: THE WREATH NEXT DOOR

This front door pick-me-up in the photo at right is easier and more forgiving to maintain than a living wreath planted in moss and soil (which requires a boatload of plants and weighs as much as a small child!). Our wreath dream weaver Jill Ellis of Makeshift Studio uses grapevine rounds as a starting point in her wildly popular workshops where the participants all start with the same materials but end up with totally different wreaths that let their personality shine through. You can do the same with the instructions on page 39.

Get the Look

- Upright rosemary hedges and hardy blueberry bushes
- Unique hydrangeas ('Limelight', oakleaf)
- Cobblestone, flagstone, and shingles

- Potted vines or topiary forms
- American flags, state flags, or stars and stripes peace sign flags
- Wicker furniture and textiles with stripes, plaids, and checks

PLAY WITH COLOR

Skew the traditional color palettes for your own spin on history. Red, white, and blue may have been your mother's mantra, but forgo the classic rouge for a hipper, hotter pink in the outdoors.

PLANT RECIPE: NEW TRADITIONAL GARDEN ▲

Vine: *Stephanotis floribunda*. **Shrubs:** *Rosmarinus officinalis* 'Tuscan Blue', *Rosa* 'Iceberg', *Hydrangea paniculata* 'Limelight', *Eucalyptus* 'Moon Lagoon', *Westringia fruticosa* 'Smokie'. **Grass:** *Leymus condensatus* 'Canyon Prince'. **Ground covers:** *Cistanthe grandiflora* 'Jazz Time', *Dymondia margaretae*, *Nepeta racemosa* 'Walker's Low'.

MAKE YOUR OWN WREATH

1. Get the Base. Grapevine wreaths come in sizes of 12 to 24 inches and can be found at most craft stores or online.

2. Get the Greens. Here fragrant eucalyptus is natural and loose with two large green *Echeveria* 'Imbricata' succulents as the stars. But any sturdy plant cuttings will work—winter pine, cypress, huckleberry, fall berries, kumquat, or pomegranate branches as well as dried persimmon or other fruit. To simplify, shop grocery store greenery! Better yet, have the kids run out and forage what's around the yard and work with what you've got.

3. Wire Them Together. Use lightweight floral wire to wrap stems and "sew" through the base of succulents and stems into the grapevine branches. Fill as much or as little of the wreath as you want. No glue. No watering. No mess. It's lightweight, easy to hang with twine, and simple to adjust for the season. Spritz with water occasionally. Voila!

Clean Minimalist

Cool, calm, and in control. From crisp outfits to streamlined interiors, it's all about good lines and flattering neutrals. Structure and style go hand-in-hand, and a clean minimalist garden should mimic those strong lines you love from the closet to the kitchen. Keep the outside equally free of clutter by using restraint and laser focus to select what goes where. When it comes to the number of plants and materials, less is more (but we probably didn't even need to tell *you* that!) for that clean, refined minimalist look.

WALK THE LINE

For a minimalist garden, design in straight lines with pavers and fencing and leave lots of negative space covered with low ground covers or turf.

CONCRETE AND WOOD

Cool concrete pavers and custom board-form concrete walls, planters, and fireplaces add modern yet timeless appeal, while wood decks, screens, and built-in benches allow the stark design to feel warm.

SOFT TOUCHES

Balance the hardscape elements with softer plant textures. Cacti and succulents and anything spiky look spot-on, but throw in fine-leafed shrubs, creeping ground covers, and a hint of color here and there so your clean minimalism doesn't read too sterile.

Get the Look

- Structured cacti, succulents, or clipped boxwood spheres
- Shades of green and silver for the plant color palette
- Pebbles for mulch
- Concrete pavers and grid layouts
- Hardwood decks and horizontal fencing
- Square containers

PLANT RECIPE: CLEAN MINIMALIST GARDEN ▶

Succulents: *Agave americana*, *Plumeria*, *Aeonium canariense*, *Echinocactus grusonii*, *Agave potatorum* 'El Camarón', *Echeveria* 'Afterglow'.

"A strong point of view keeps you from overfilling and cluttering up tight spaces."

KEEP IT CLEAN AND GREEN WITH AN OUTDOOR SHOWER GARDEN

Calling all surfers at heart! East Coast to West Coast and everyone in between can enjoy an outdoor shower—a vacation in itself during the summer months and practical for hosing off kids, dogs, and yourself after full summer days. Match your shower to your style—modern horizontal slats, brass fixtures, and Turkish towels— and it's suddenly the hippest part of the house. Take it one step further by planting around the shower pad with selections that will thrive with intermittent heavy "rainfall" to create a living border for your watery slice of heaven. Our picks for the best "set it and forget it" shower plants are giant velvet rose (*Aeonium canariense*), asparagus fern (*Asparagus densiflorus* 'Myers'), frangipani (*Plumeria*), golden Japanese forest grass (*Hakonechloa macra* 'Aureola'), dwarf golden sweet flag (*Acorus gramineus* 'Minimus Aureus') and 'Silver Falls' dichondra (*Dichondra argentea* 'Silver Falls').

Global Boho

Call it the *Eat, Pray, Love* Garden. Create your favorite (or fantasy) getaway with a garden room that satisfies your wanderlust without ever leaving home. Channel your carefree, bohemian spirit by layering greenery and textiles and travel souvenirs. Scout vintage and thrift stores for accessories; this vintage carved daybed that the owner calls the "Wizard Bed" was found at a resale shop and immediately sends us spinning to the Far East, even for just twenty minutes on a Tuesday. Toss in splashes of vivid color, found objects (maybe that Buddha statue you've been lugging around for years), comfy floor poufs, and enough soft candlelight to start dreaming about that next trip.

HIGHLIGHT YOUR SUPERSTAR

Add a tree that can grow long-term in a planter for height and visual interest. Choose a special variety that reminds you of a trip—signal that magical week in Cabo with a blue fan palm (*Brahea armata*) or pot a dragon's blood tree (*Dracaena draco*) to honor that once-in-a-lifetime journey to Morocco.

ADD TEXTURE AND PATTERN

Rugs and pillows are great ways to pull tribal designs into your outdoor rooms. Mix and match your plant textures for a living tapestry of patterns. Long and spikey, tall and weepy, loose and leafy—go for variety with an assortment of plants and containers.

GET GROUNDED

Low slung is the way to go. Think plush poufs or floor pillows at ground level. Low seating evokes a connection to the Earth and is the preferred way people from many non-Western cultures dine, entertain, and relax. Don't be afraid of using indoor pieces outdoors for areas with dry summers—the result is downright liberating!

Get the Look

- Houseplants for protected spaces with stands to mix heights
- Spanish moss (living or dried) hung for moody texture
- Earthy and jewel tones
- Grounded poufs, garden daybed, pillows, and rugs for seating
- Bowl with floating candles and water plants
- LED lights for extra magic

PLANT RECIPE: GLOBAL BOHO GARDEN ▶

Containers: *Brahea armata, Dracaena marginata, Euphorbia trigona, Zamioculcas zamiifolia, Neoregelia carolinae, Ficus elastica* 'Burgundy', *Cordyline* 'Jurred', *Pistia stratiotes, Peperomia obtusifolia*. **Hanging:** *Tillandsia usneoides*.

FIRE + WATER

This age-old pair of yin and yang works as an easy fire and water feature: an antique Tibetan singing bowl is filled with floating candles and a vintage Chinese egg pot holds water lettuce (*Pistia stratiotes*). Votives, LED twinkle lights, and string lights add a meditative glow to the garden.

BIG BOX SHOPPING FOR A FARAWAY LOOK

We love local garden shops. In fact, we have our nursery phone numbers on speed dial. But sometimes a trip to the hardware store or your local big box retailer (we're not naming names) can do just the trick. For this garden, we found some of our favorite oldies-but-goodies, including the ponytail palm (*Beaucarnea recurvata*), mother-in-law's tongue (not ours!) (*Sansevieria trifasciata* 'Variegata'), and burgundy rubber plant (*Ficus elastica* 'Burgundy'). They easily mix and mingle with more exotic finds, such as the Mexican blue fan palm (*Brahea armata*)— cue the margaritas! Just like your closet, shop high-low and don't be afraid to mix it all together.

Color Play

Yes, you like piña coladas and getting caught in the rain! Life is vibrant at every turn and your wardrobe and home reflect your sunny outlook on life. Likewise, the garden should be anything but monochromatic. Color your outdoor world for a fun everyday adventure that makes a great backdrop to those birthdays and milestones you love to celebrate. Find a winning palette inspired by your favorite shirt or the peppy paint on your front door and work in plants to follow that shade. Layering and repetition is key here to mass tones together for a color story that looks well thought out rather than an explosion of rainbow sprinkles.

LIVING FOCAL POINT

Choose one extra-large plant or tree with an interesting shape. A strawberry tree (*Arbutus marina*) or gray century plant (*Agave americana*) offers a leading-lady wow factor that complements the cast of brighter, smaller plants.

CONTAIN IN COLOR

Choose containers to set inside the garden in shades that complement your palette. Skip terra-cotta, white, and black basics and opt for glossy finishes and vibrant colors. The glazed turquoise blue picks up the natural teal blues and greens of the plants.

PLAY WITH CURVES

Rather than a straight beeline, the arching bend in the path softens the tinted concrete and gives guests more time to meander through the garden. This creates a playful and inviting entrance.

Get the Look

- Large gray agave or silver-leafed tree as focal point
- Tall, showy plants such as ornamental grasses and perennials with upright, sword-shaped leaves
- Colorful ground covers
- Large glazed colorful pots in shades of teal and turquoise
- Bright tilework
- Neon mesh Acapulco chairs

PLANT RECIPE: COLOR PLAY GARDEN ▶

Trees: *Arbutus* 'Marina', *Olea europea* 'Wilsonii'. **Succulents:** *Agave attenuata, Agave americana.* **Medium perennials:** *Anigozanthos* 'Harmony', *Phormium* 'Maori Queen'. **Grasses:** *Leymus condensatus* 'Canyon Prince', *Nassella tenuissima. Festuca glauca* 'Elijah Blue', *Sesleria autumnalis.* **Ground covers:** *Senecio mandraliscae, Graptopetalum paraguayense, Sedum nussbaumerianum, Dymondia margaretae.*

DREAM IN COLOR

A daybed is an unexpected statement piece, focal point, and literal reminder that gardens are meant to help us relax and renew. Different styles of garden loungers easily take us around the world—rattan feels like a trip to breezy Bali, carved mahogany evokes an African safari, vintage iron takes us to a French chateau. This hanging garden bed is secured by thick nautical ropes to an overhead trellis, where the flowering vines are allowed to twine. Cushions, pillows, throws, and an outdoor rug give it luxe layers that transform a beige courtyard into an outdoor dream.

Old World

Paris or Rome? The eternal question. If you're the type that's always dreaming of a trip to Europe, it's high time you brought that feeling home. Anchor the space with timeless trees and layer the table with vintage linens and hand-dipped candlesticks. String up the lights and cue Edith Piaf. Whether it's France or Italy, you can have Old World rustic luxe at home with a few easy adds and plants that are small garden takes on the big classics. Start collecting terra-cotta pots from yard sales and your mom's garage—the more weathered the better. Fill with herbs such as rosemary and lavender, and the fragrance will have you dreaming of Provence in no time.

LOOK DOWN

What's underfoot? For a very small patio or yard, clean and functional hardscape is the first choice. Brick and stone give the feel of a villa but even easy (read cheap) gravel will get you traveling back in time faster than concrete or wood decks.

ENCLOSE THE SPACE

Height and texture will help you and your friends sink into conversation like a big Italian family. If you have trees in place, nestle your table under their canopy; if not, plant trees in pots to create your own cozy grove.

LIGHT THE WAY

Part of this romantic style comes from lighting. Hang string lights overhead and layer in cool candelabras. A chiminea in the background looks like another terra-cotta pot but gives the glow of an outdoor fireplace and is a quick, affordable way to spark up a small space.

Get the Look

- Olive trees—inherited or in nursery crates, or use mini olive tree seedlings as centerpieces
- Fragrant white roses, rosemary, lavender, and jasmine
- Terra-cotta planters
- String lights
- Natural linen, rattan furniture, brass candlesticks, glass carafes, wooden cheeseboards

PLANT RECIPE: OLD WORLD GARDEN ▶

Trees: *Cupressus sempervirens* 'Monshel', *Citrus × limon* 'Eureka', *Olea europaea*. **Vines:** *Bougainvillea* 'James Walker'. **Shrubs:** *Lavandula stoechas* 'Otto Quast', *Pittosporum crassifolium* 'Compactum', *Olea europaea* 'Montra'. **Ground covers:** *Convolvulus sabatius*, *Dichondra argentea* 'Silver Falls', *Teucrium ackermannii*.

GARDEN PARTY!

Style your table—naturally. Plant what you love and plan on pruning before your parties for fast table decor. Quick snips of branches, leaves, and loose flowers add fresh style to the dinner table. We love lavender for the color and fragrance, olive branches for the symbolism and Old World style, and white roses—they smell great and work with just about any look or party theme!

INSTANT ORCHARD

Friends are coming Saturday night for an outdoor dinner party, but the garden still feels like a cold, concrete jungle. In your head you've been picturing a dreamy vineyard-inspired dinner outside with a long farm table and friends laughing late into the night by flattering candlelight. But that's so not the case. *Help!*

We've been there, with little time to turn realistic conditions into that dream scenario. When your outdoor space is light on heritage trees and heavy on uninspired hardscape (something that's not changing anytime soon), there is a fast fix (and we're not talking about plane tickets to Napa). We call it the Instant Orchard! Here we overnighted four boxed olive trees and kept them in their cheerful stamped wooden nursery crates. We placed the trees at the four corners of the patio, tucked tight to the table, to create instant intimacy, close conversation, and romance—be it for a big bash or Sunday breakfast for two.

FIND THE BOX TREE THAT'S BEST FOR YOU

Olive trees evoke that Old World vineyard feel, but if you want a different look or need cold-climate choices, there are many other patio trees suited to their wooden crates. (The crated trees are called "box trees" in the trade and come in 24-inch, 36-inch, and larger sizes).

- Trees that grow well long-term in boxes are slow-growers with compact root systems.

- Most need regular organic fertilizer and water (more in hot months). It's best to put your tree on an automatic drip irrigation system—set it and forget it!

- Box trees can be ordered and delivered through your garden store or sourced from a wholesale nursery by your gardener.

- Ask your tree vendor about the water needs and longevity of the particular tree you choose that grows in your region. Certain trees outgrow their space faster than others and may need to be repotted into larger containers or into the ground.

- A 24-inch box tree can be moved by hand with one or two strong gardeners and a dolly. Larger sizes may require machinery and special equipment. Check with your installer before going bigger than 24 inches.

- Best Box-Tree Bets: Fruitless olive (*Olea europaea* 'Wilsonii'), Black Mission fig (*Ficus carica* 'Mission'), 'Little Gem' magnolia (*Magnolia grandiflora* 'Little Gem'), privet (*Ligustrum*), small conifers, palo verde (*Parkinsonia aculeata*), bay laurel (*Laurus nobilis*), crape myrtle (*Lagerstroemia indica*), and Japanese maple (*Acer palmatum*).

2

SMALL GARDEN DESIGN SCHOOL

In a petite space, the whole garden can be taken in with one look around. It is therefore even more important to thoughtfully design small gardens as a cohesive whole to create restful and elegant environments. So pull up a chair and get cozy! We're bringing the best of design school to you, and tuition is free. Don't worry, this is not traditional Landscape Architecture 101, where you spend late nights in the computer lab laboring over your 3D renderings. This is a crash course in field-tested, fundamental design principles (and our day-to-day secret tricks) that make their way into magazines and client's hearts.

We'll start high, with the essential ingredients of visual design, so we can get low (down-in-the-dirt low) with photos of real gardens and containers to see design principles in action. Drawing on both our backgrounds in graphic design and magazine layout, we'll teach you how to see outdoor spaces first as graphic compositions— using what we call "The Fantastic Five."

THE FANTASTIC FIVE DESIGN PRINCIPLES

1. Line + Space

2. Focal Point

3. Eye Candy
   (Color, Shape + Form, Texture)

4. Layering + Repetition

5. Contrast

Mastering the Fantastic Five will give you newfound confidence and steer you in the right design direction before you worry a hot second about which plants to pick. This approach works especially well in the small garden where you can see the whole "page" in one glance.

Line + Space

Like an old house, every garden with "good bones" has an underlying structure that helps the garden relate to the home's architecture. These bones are the line and space layout that ensure good flow between the different outdoor zones. Clearly defining our spaces creates a comfortable sense of enclosure. A space that is too empty (even if it's small) can feel cold and uninviting, yet a space too compact and cluttered can feel chaotic and claustrophobic. When laying out a new garden, a few line and space tricks direct us where to start and stop and how to connect pathways, patios, and planter beds.

CONNECT THE DOTS

Put simply, the garden should relate to the house. The edges and corners of the home (that is, windows, doors, and porches) should line up, connect, and balance the edges of patios, pathways, and planters.

CHOOSE A GRID OR CURVED LAYOUT

Choose the corresponding line or curve approach that matches your style. A geometric grid layout (squares and rectangles) feels structured and modern. A curved layout (winding arcs and circles) reads more informal and natural. You can modernize the look of a garden with square patios and rectangular pavers, or soften a modern look by adding curved pathways and planter beds. Mother Nature, the master gardener, designs in curves, so even the most contemporary gardens should include some circles, curved edges, or rounded plantings.

BALANCE: SYMMETRY + ASYMMETRY

Balance creates harmony in the garden by arranging symmetrical or asymmetrical elements. A symmetrical landscape layout means that elements on one side of the garden mirror the elements on the other side—best for formal or traditional styles. Asymmetrical layouts enhance modern *and* organic designs and have more freedom to add creative surprises.

POSITIVE + NEGATIVE SPACE

Equally important, positive space refers to the solid elements, such as shrubs or furniture, that fill the garden, while negative space is the "empty" background that helps highlight the positive. In the garden, the negative space is often the livable space— lawn, gravel patio, concrete pavers, wood deck—that creates literal breathing room.

PLAYING WITH PROPORTION + SCALE

Scale is architect-speak for size relative to its surrounding environment. Proportion is how one object relates to others and the setting. A tiny bistro table might look like dollhouse furniture under a huge old oak tree, but it will be perfectly proportioned on your small balcony.

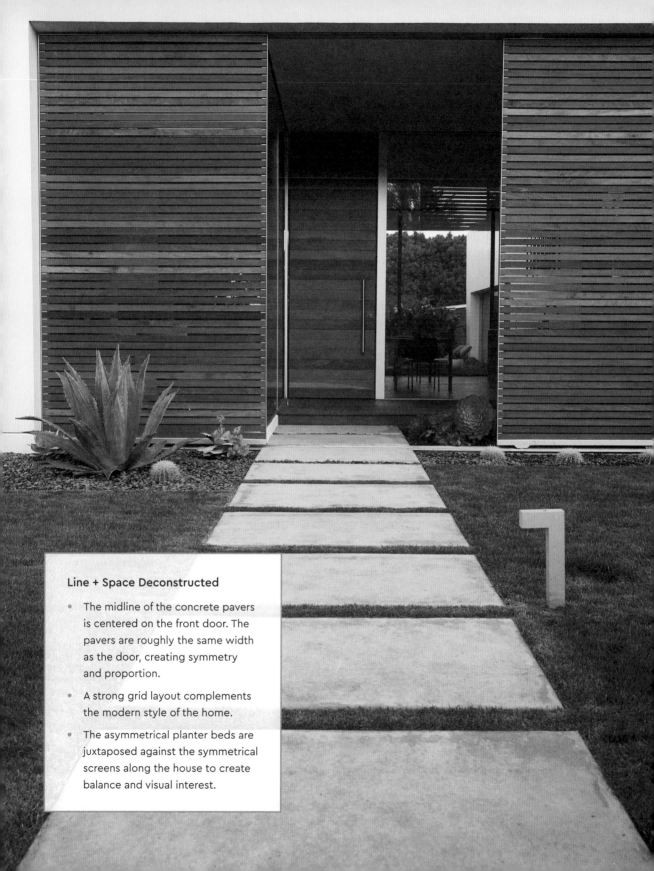

Line + Space Deconstructed

- The midline of the concrete pavers is centered on the front door. The pavers are roughly the same width as the door, creating symmetry and proportion.

- A strong grid layout complements the modern style of the home.

- The asymmetrical planter beds are juxtaposed against the symmetrical screens along the house to create balance and visual interest.

Focal Point

A focal point draws attention to a specific point in the garden by catching the eye with color, contrast, and scale. It can beckon you to a destination at the end of a pathway, call you to a seating area, and make your small space feel bigger by stretching your line of vision to the boundaries of the garden. Stretch that sightline even further by framing a distant mountain view with two trees planted in your garden. Containers are the easiest way to add an instant focal point, such as this "faux fountain" (pictured at right) that has trailing plants that drip down like water. Size is important—too small and you might miss it, but too big or too many and the focal point can overwhelm small spaces or become a distraction. Three is a magic garden number and keep it as a max for focal points.

TYPES OF FOCAL POINTS

- Trees
- Water features
- Fire pits
- Containers
- Views

Focal Point Deconstructed ▶

- The bright turquoise of the container catches the eye and is the most vibrant color in the garden.

- The simple circle of low green ground cover at the base of the container focuses attention on the tall container rising above it.

- The structural agave makes a statement, but does not block the view of the seating area in the distance.

◀ **Design Tip:** Don't forget the view from inside the house—plant trees or place containers in outdoor spots where you can enjoy them from the window and as you enter or exit.

PLANT RECIPE: FAUX FOUNTAIN CONTAINER ▶

Succulents: *Agave celsii* 'Nova', *Sedum clavatum*, *Senecio radicans*. **Ground cover:** *Geranium × cantabrigiense* 'Biokovo'.

Eye Candy (Color, Shape + Form, Texture)

Whether you're painting a landscape or planting a garden, every creative project needs a little eye candy. Color, shape, form, and texture take good to great.

COLOR

The artist's color wheel is a secret weapon for a perfect palette. It groups harmonious colors next to each other by hue with warm reds, oranges, and yellows on one side and cool greens, blues, and purples on the other. You can't go wrong if you stick to one side of the wheel with warms or cools. Or match colors across from each other on the wheel to create contrast, such as orange with blue or yellow with purple. Unlike the painting metaphor, most plants in the garden have green leaves which add a reliable base layer of cool green, whether you run hot or cold.

TONES FOR MOOD AND STYLE

Color evokes feelings and can alter our perception of the space around us. Warm, hot, bright colors evoke energy, excitement, and passion. Yet using lots of warm, bright colors in the small garden can make the space feel even smaller. Too many different contrasting colors can make you feel on edge. Cool, muted colors induce relaxation and calm and can make a space feel bigger. Color is also related to personal style, but since natural, organic hues are so different from interiors and textile colors, it's good to stay open-minded. You might not purchase a purple dress or armchair but you just might love that color in your blooming morning glories (*Ipomoea purpurea*) or Mexican sage (*Salvia leucantha* 'Santa Barbara'). One splash of unexpected, living color can draw attention to your favorite part of the garden.

COLOR PALETTES

Choose a color palette and stick to it for a cohesive garden look. Contrast lights and darks (in any color) to keep things interesting. For example, a monochromatic blue color palette can vary the shades from light silver and aqua to deep ocean cobalt.

▶ **Design Tip:** Nothing grabs our attention in the garden as much as colorful blooms, yet most flowers are fleeting. Bring year-round color into the garden with ground covers and shrubs that have shades of silver, blue, lime, and white, as well as purple and orange foliage.

PLANT RECIPE: SUCCULENT COURTYARD ▶

Ground covers: *Echeveria* 'Perle Von Nürnberg', *Echeveria elegans*, *Dymondia margaretae*, *Senecio serpens*, *Sedum rupestre* 'Angelina', *Aloe* 'Rooikappie'. **Medium succulents:** *Senecio cylindricustalinoides* subsp. *cylindricus*, *Agave attenuata*. **Container:** *Agave desmettiana* 'Variegata'. **Espalier:** *Grewia occidentalis*.

EASY CENTERPIECE
Forage the garden for
a fast centerpiece of
warm and bright citrus
contrasted with cool
succulent snips.

Warm colors

Contrasting light and dark colors

Cool colors

Bright colors

SHAPE + FORM

Shape is the two-dimensional outline (patio, pathway, wire trellis pattern) while form is the three-dimensional outline (how a plant or tree looks in its space). Plant forms can include upright, bushy, fountain, cascading, trunked, columnar, and spreading. Contrasting or coordinating groups of plant forms create interest. For example, pairing three different kinds of fountain grasses makes for an overall coordinated look that is light and flowing. Grouping four different kinds of green foundation shrubs is dense and rounded.

▲ **Design Tip:** An L-shaped seat wall creates a welcoming entry courtyard. Staggered wood or concrete benches can also conjure the same feeling of stepping into a special part of the garden.

> ### Shape + Form Deconstructed ▶
>
> - The monochromatic tones are muted, but plant shapes and forms create powerful contrast. The Little Ollie (*Olea europaea* 'Montra') is bushy and full; the string of fishhooks (*Senecio radicans*) is cascading and delicate; and the donkey's tail (*Sedum morganianum*) is spilling and dense.
>
> - The upright urn-shaped container contrasts with the round, bushy, and cascading plant forms.

Design Tip: This original 1920s brick was repurposed and relaid from running bond (subway) pattern to herringbone to create an updated look with maximum texture.

TEXTURE

All good garden designs include a mix of contrasting plant and hardscape textures and pattern. Visual texture relates to the way a plant looks, not feels. A golden barrel cactus looks furry from a distance, but its sharp spikes appear up close. Hardscape textures refer to both how a surface looks and feels. Brick floors or pebbles may look rough, but feel smooth under your feet. The three main plant textures—coarse, medium, and fine—are defined by their leaf size, shape, and direction. Coarse-texture plants have big leaves or spaces between the leaves. They command attention and should be used sparingly in the small garden; otherwise it could start to feel like a jungle. But if a tropical, resort getaway is the look you crave, then large, coarse-textured plants, such as palms and philodendrons, will do the trick. Fine-textured plants are lacy and airy, such as a ground cover.

Smooth

Soft

◄ **Texture Deconstructed**

A The fine texture of the Kurapia ground cover (*Lippia nodiflora* 'Kurapia') contrasts with the coarse textures of the background palm leaves.

B The coarse palms include (left-to-right) Canary Island date palm (*Phoenix canariensis*), queen palm (*Syagrus romanzoffiana*), and king palm (*Archontophoenix cunninghamiana*).

C The Santa Rosa plum tree shows off its medium texture leaves.

D The herringbone brick (reset on its skinny edge) reinforces the texture and patterns of the awning, throw pillows, and welcome mat.

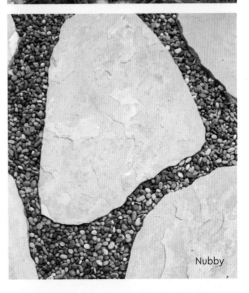

Nubby

Layering + Repetition

Layering creates depth in the garden. Creating different visual planes of varying size and scale makes us feel like the garden extends beyond the first row of plantings. And let's talk about that row. Unless you're going for an ultramodern look, your plants should not be like *Madeline* in two straight lines, rain or shine. Stagger your groups into drifts (like snow) and stack them with the shorter ground covers and smaller accent plants up front, extending to the medium shrubs in the middle, and larger shrubs and hedges at the back. Add a few trees and feature plants sprinkled in to mix up the scale.

Repetition is used with plant and hardscape design to create a unified look—a series of matching concrete planters, a neat row of identical orange aloes, groups of red salvia throughout the garden, or a mass of one ornamental grass. It's always stronger to repeat fewer different types of plants rather than scattering a little of this and a little of that.

Layering + Repetition Deconstructed ▶

A   Hybrid coral aloes (*Aloe striata × maculata*) with blue leaves tucked in a bed of blue chalksticks (*Senecio mandraliscae*) ground cover are repeated across the slope.

B   A layer of citrus trees repeated behind the aloes adds height and scale.

C   The repetition of plants combined with layering creates cohesion and strong textural contrast.

"It's always stronger to repeat fewer different types of plants than scattering a little of this and a little of that."

Contrast

Contrast in form, texture, color, and value is fundamental in garden design! It is the foundation to creating visual interest. From hardscape layout to material selection to plant design, contrast should be front and center in every design decision. Whether your personal style is dramatic high-contrast or subtle monochromatic, contrasting values (lights and darks) are a must. In the whimsical color garden, opposing yellows and purples create color contrast. In the monochromatic garden, only one color is used, but contrast shows up in textures and value. Contrasting shapes are a quick way to play with this principle; try round containers on the edge of a square patio or mix airy chairs with dense furniture. Every element can create contrast if you work your opposites.

WAYS TO CREATE CONTRAST IN THE SMALL GARDEN

- Sink solid boulders in masses of soft, feathery grasses.
- Plant a tall blooming tree at the corner of a gravel dining area to create height contrast.
- Connect two square brick patios with a curving flagstone pathway.
- Paint a picket fence black to contrast with a white farmhouse.
- Soften the edge of a concrete porch with a mass of fuzzy lamb's ear (*Stachys byzantina* 'Helen von Stein').
- Train an espalier jasmine vine (*Trachelospermum jasminoides*) with dark green leaves up a white wall.
- Nest a silver spiky agave in a mat of green rosemary ground cover.
- Group plants with different forms (upright, spiky, fountain, mounded, spilling, creeping, and so on) in one container.

Design Tip: White commands the most attention and should either be used sparingly in the small garden or repeated for an all white-and-green garden. White, light green, and silver can also brighten up shady spots. If you want a corner to disappear, stick with greens.

The Fantastic Five, Deconstructed ▶

Here's how Line + Space, Focal Point, Eye Candy, Layering + Repetition, and Contrast get pulled into this garden.

- The fire pit stars as a strong **focal point,** drawing your eye to the center of the "room" and conjuring up images of intimate gatherings. It's surrounded by a lush ground cover that softens the concrete edges and creates a carpet of irresistible, contrasting **eye candy (texture).**

- The garden **space** has a modern asymmetrical (un-matchy) layout, balanced with oval accent chairs and container groupings.

- The **scale** of the 3-foot-wide fire pit is grounded by an oversized sectional.

- Light and dark grays give **contrast** and are **repeated** on the fire pit, the horizontal fence, the furniture, and geometric throw pillows.

- Dark Mexican river pebbles and light flagstone "flooring" add barefoot-friendly **contrasting texture** and graphic pattern.

- The **layer** of blooming 'Slim' bottlebrush hedges (*Callistemon viminalis* 'Slim') along the fence adds shade and visual depth in the background. The succulent containers are grouped in different sizes and shapes, but the **repeated** use of the terra-cotta keeps things cohesive.

PLANT RECIPE: BOLD ECLECTIC CITY GARDEN

Tree: *Olea europea* 'Swan Hill'. **Tall:** *Callistemon viminalis* 'Slim'. **Medium:** *Salvia chamaedryoides* x 'Marine Blue'. **Ground cover:** *Thymus serpyllum*, *Delosperma nubigenum*, and *Sesleria caerulea*. **Container Plants:** *Echeveria* 'Afterglow', *Echeveria agavoides* 'Lipstick', *Cordyline australis* 'Torbay Dazzler', *Sedum nussbaumerianun*, *Graptosedum* 'Darley Sunshine', *Oscularia deltoides*.

3

SMALL GARDEN FLOORS, WALLS, AND CEILINGS

A welcoming presence, a place to chat, a spot for a book or drink, a pretty centerpiece. Creating an outdoor room is much like our interiors—it's combining beauty and comfort on the three planes of floors (function), walls (privacy), and ceilings (shade). And we love to call our small gardens outdoor "rooms" because they really are living, *livable* spaces where we take our favorite indoor activities—dining, entertaining, playing, and relaxing—outside and closer to nature while still feeling cozy and at home.

Coziness, that sense of being comfortably contained, is what makes a small garden feel enchanting. Using the same rules of interior design, planning the outdoor room from floor to wall to ceiling creates a space that is not only nice to look at but also comfortable to spend time in. In a small garden it's important to balance enclosure with openness so that your small space stays cozy but not overly confined.

Easy, Affordable Floors

No one wants to walk around on dirt. Garden floors of patios and pathways provide a stable and clean surface for walking and lounging. The materials you select will also help set the tone for your garden style. With such a huge range of cost and complexity—everything from imported Italian quarried marble to woodchips to prefab pavers—there is much to choose from. Here's a breakdown of our favorite easy floor options for decks, paths, lawns, and patios.

DOWN THE DRAIN

In general, loose, permeable floors (like gravel) are the most casual and least expensive. They also allow water to pass through and drain naturally.

GREEN FLOORS: STAKE YOUR TURF

The great American lawn is shrinking due to space, water, and resource constraints. Don't get us wrong, a little grass that gets used by people, pets, and kids is not a crime. Lawns help cool the feet and air and provide visual relief in the garden. However, faux grass and sod grass alternatives are worth considering for many reasons. Traditional lawns with traditional turf grasses are water-, labor-, and fertilizer-intensive and are really meant to grow wild in English gardens (in England)!

FAUX GRASS

Artificial turf has come a long way since it was introduced as a fluorescent green patch at the RV park. Many of the new products are more lifelike and long-lasting and work great for dry regions, high-traffic spaces, or areas that are difficult to access for weekly mowing. Acres of fake grass will look, well, fake, but small areas of artificial turf work especially well in the small garden and tend to look more realistic.

REAL GRASS ALTERNATIVES

Hybrid Bermuda grass, such as Tifgreen (we plant it all the time in Southern California), along with buffalo grass (*Buchloe dactyloides*) can grow in cooler climates, use half the water of traditional turf grasses,

Kurapia

Artificial turf

Pea gravel

LIVING ROOM LOUNGE

An ipe wood deck floor and a layered wall of soft shrubs in front of the fence warm an otherwise minimal space. This area is left intentionally sunny with a blue-sky ceiling for warmer afternoons in a cool, coastal garden.

and stay greener in the winter. Our new favorite grass alternative is the bright green Kurapia (*Lippia nodiflora* 'Kurapia') ground cover that looks and acts like grass but has roots that grow 10 feet deep and require half the water. Plus, Kurapia's leaves and white flowers only need mowing once a season. With so many options, you can get creative and ditch the lawn that's just for looks.

TIPS FOR SUCCESSFUL ARTIFICIAL TURF

- Hire a reputable installer who will ensure the grade, grass grain, and borders are prepared and installed correctly. Request to visit one of their projects that's at least a year old to see the work first-hand.

- Use sand infill on top of the turf that's regular, nontoxic play sand or odor resistant organic infill for pets (not rubber pellets).

- Install turf in an area with some shade or plant trees for future shade (turf gets hot!).

- Turf works great in a rectangular layout for a modern style, and even better with irregular curving edges.

- Cut natural boulders into the curves and corners to break up the lines.

- Plant *real* ornamental grasses at the edges of the turf to trick the eye. Check out our favorite small ornamental grasses on page 176.

Floor Materials

- Flagstone + ground cover: Select stone that looks like naturally occurring stone in your area and fill the spaces with silver carpet (*Dymondia margaretae*) ground cover.

- Brick: What is old is new again. A herringbone pattern set on the skinny edge (pictured at right) updates a classic pattern and material.

- Mulch: Many cities have green recycling programs that offer free or low-cost mulch.

- Wood deck: Decks can add warmth, solve slope challenges, and be built by handy homeowners. Wood decks need to be sanded and stained annually to keep them looking good, so make sure you're willing to spend spring Saturdays tending the deck.

- Concrete pavers + ground cover: Custom poured-in-place concrete pavers give maximum design flexibility, but prefab pavers in a variety of sizes are readily available and work great with Kurapia (*Lippia nodiflora* 'Kurapia') planted in between.

- Gravel + perimeter planting: High-impact and weekend-friendly. Prepare the base layer with 2 to 3 inches of compacted (weed-free) soil or road base with only ½ to 1 inch of gravel on top. You'll be tempted to skip the base layer and just add more gravel, but the result will be squishy and hard to walk on. Soften the edges with creeping myoporum (*Myoporum parvifolium* 'Putah Creek'), which adds green but can't be stepped on directly.

ROCK YOUR FLOORS—
WITH NATURAL BOULDERS!

Boulders add gravitas and timeless beauty to the outdoor room and can be built right into the floor. Boulders can connect your garden to its environment when you use stone that is naturally occurring in your area. Well-placed boulders can also give a new garden a sense of permanence.

TIPS FOR GARDENING
WITH BOULDERS

- Group boulders as they occur in nature in clusters of threes or more or as a single large statement.

- Think of boulders as icebergs. Bury them one-half to two-thirds *below* the soil so they look "moved in" and don't appear as though they were dropped down yesterday. You might be tempted to roll them around and let them lie like sun-tanning seals, but they belong partially submerged, just like icebergs!

- Bring in the biggest size stones that you or your gardener can move. Bigger is usually better, especially since you will lose half their visible height underground.

Boulders also make beautiful, natural water features. Unlike traditional fountains that have an underground basin, pump, and electrical outlet, a water "bath" can rely on rainwater or the garden hose. This water feature is both a birdbath, doggy refresher,

and a basin to float flowers and candles. Far from a kitschy focal point, a natural rock birdbath is a subtle surprise in the garden.

HOW TO CREATE A
BOULDER BIRDBATH

Use a boulder on site with a natural depression or purchase a suitable boulder. Bury your boulder one-half to two-thirds deep (remember the iceberg!) For our boulder, we hired a stone mason for two hours of labor to saw-cut and hand-chip the basin.

Other ways to get this look (without a chisel) include using a metal, stone, clay, or concrete bowl and nestling it within the landscape, directly on the ground.

Walls We Love—Hedges, Fences + Planters

With your "floor" plan in place, let's take a look at the walls. Walls create that cozy sense of enclosure in your contained garden. Get creative and choose the right scale for your small space. Remember, size matters—too much wall can dominate a small garden and cue the claustrophobia.

Determine what kind of wall you want. It can be something built or it can be a few simple containers of potted trees or tall plants to give you that much needed room definition. Don't forget to talk to your neighbors before you move, build, or change any walls or fences on property lines. Also, check local codes and verify property lines and setbacks with professional surveyors or certified site plans.

▲ **CONTAIN YOURSELF**
Little Ollies (*Olea europaea* 'Montra') can live almost indefinitely in containers with good drainage, regular water, and fertilizer. This instant wall barrier makes an open stairwell edge safer.

WALL TYPES & MATERIALS

- Wood or metal fences

- Traditional walls (stone, brick, stucco, concrete)

- Living walls

- Wood landscape timbers (clean railroad ties)

- Lines of containers filled with tall plants

- Hedges

INSTANT WALLS

One of the easiest and fastest ways to make a wall on top of existing hardscape is to create a container wall using repeated containers and plantings. This technique works great near stairs or next to a ledge as an easy solution to divide one space into different zones or to screen features that you want to disappear. Poof!

▲ RETHINK THE WALL

Whenever possible, natural and green screening, such as this dry-stack gravity stone wall with a bougainvillea vine, is almost always prettier than looking at a wood fence!

STYLE SECRET

Soften your walls and floors with plants. If you have the luxury of designing from scratch, look for ways to create planter pockets and cut-outs that soften and define your outdoor zones and focal points. The Mexican gem succulent (*Echeveria elegans*) and dwarf mondo grass (*Ophiopogon japonicus* 'Nana') in this photo soften the edge of a board-form concrete wall of a fire pit.

GREEN WALLS

Quick vertical gardening and living walls have been a garden trend for a while now, and the best part is that they can be done easily or extravagantly. For a really small space—think accent or divider walls—simple ceramic wall containers (see page 26) or woolly pockets can hold splashes of greenery, succulents, or herbs. For a five-minute hack, grab a few nails or hooks and hang some draping tillandsia (see page 45) with a piece of string or wire—cheap green thrills! Espalier takes a touch more time, but is surprisingly easy and incredibly elegant.

THE EASY ART OF ESPALIER

Espalier (pronounced es-spal-yay) is the *très chic* French art of training trees and plants to grow flat and vertically. It may sound fancy, but it translates to tying branches against their trellis and chopping off any branch that dares to stick out at you and away from the wall (take that!). It's a unique way to cover a large wall or fence and give some high interest without relying on a bulky hedge—a boon for the small garden where space is at a premium.

GARDEN UP: PATTERNED VINES

For a trellis shaped in a classic diamond (Belgian fence) pattern (shown at right), use wire and secure vines with clear plastic garden tape. Or, create a modern parallel horizontal or vertical pattern for the espalier to follow. It really is like the trend of wallpapering just one wall for a standout accent, but this one is living, wild, and one of a kind!

TOP FIVE PATTERN-MAKERS

1. Star jasmine (*Trachelospermum jasminoides*)

2. Lavender star flower (*Grewia occidentalis*)

3. Pink powder puff tree (*Calliandra haematocephala*)

4. Fruiting trees and plants: citrus, fig, apple, pear, grape

5. Azalea (*Rhododendron*)

(See page 175 for more recommended pattern-makers.)

Ceiling Canopies

Garden ceilings can add shade, beauty, and a protected feeling to small spaces. Shielding the elements extends outdoor living later into the evening and season. Built structures, such as pergolas or trellises, provide the framework for integrated lights and heaters. But adding a garden ceiling does not have to be costly or complicated. Trees make the best ceilings by providing shade and seasonal interest, plus they look great glowing with string lights or lanterns.

SEVEN EASY BEAUTIFUL CEILINGS FOR THE SMALL GARDEN

1. Place your seating area under an existing tree, or even under the canopy of a neighbor's tree that extends over your fence.

2. Plant a new tree, or a few. Notice how the sun hits your space and choose the tree location so that it blocks the rays during the times you'll be outside.

3. Add an umbrella or two, either a colorful, stationary market umbrella or a swing umbrella that can move with the sun. Both have a small footprint.

4. Hang a shade sail attached to the corners of your house and a third point, such as a fence. This is great for a narrow side garden.

5. Build a wood or metal trellis and plant it with vines for a natural layer above.

6. Install a canvas awning (awnings have come a long way since the vintage accordion metal versions).

7. Add string lights for the ultimate quick-fix ceiling with a romantic glow.

4

TOP-TO-BOTTOM
PLANT SELECTION

Choosing plants can feel daunting, especially for a small space where everything is within eyesight and every choice matters. Our foolproof approach works from tallest to smallest plants and keeps *contrast* at the forefront of each selection.

Designing high to low and incorporating varying heights of plants is vital to creating a layered look in a small garden and is an easy way to start your design. Even though we start tall with the trees, the small ground covers and succulents that are viewed at close range are just as important. Choosing plants with contrasting color, value, texture, and form ensures that your plant palette stays fresh and interesting. And last, but not least, selecting plants that will thrive in your region and in the specific conditions of your garden will save frustration and money and keep your garden looking good for the long term.

High-to-Low Design

A no-fail small garden is composed of highs and lows (just like real life).

- Highest: Trees
- High: Vines and tall shrubs (hedges)
- Medium: Medium evergreen shrubs, medium flowering perennials, and grasses
- Low: Ground covers + small succulents

Use this for a rule of thumb while shopping: Choose no more than one or two types of trees, one type of vine, one or two types of tall shrubs, three to five types of medium shrubs, one or two types of perennials, one or two types of grasses, and one or two types of ground covers. Here are the steps you'll take to put these categories together to fit your style and space:

Step 1: Think about your garden and plant style, based on your quiz results (see page 15).

Step 2: Assess the light conditions of the different areas of your garden (sunny, partly sunny, or shady) and as you select your plants, make sure their light requirements match the areas where you intend to put them (light requirements can be found on the plant tags or online).

Step 3: Select the first plant in each height category.

Step 4: Pick companion plants in each height category that contrast with your first plant in terms of texture, form, and value (light and dark).

Step 5: Make a photo collage of your plant picks to make sure you've got a mix that makes you happy.

Plant Selection Pitfalls

You heard it here, don't do this!

- **Don't focus on blooms over leaves.** Flowers fizzle. Foliage, a fancy term for leaves, is the dominant characteristic of a plant and what you notice first. Choose plants with foliage of different shapes, textures, colors, and values.

- **Don't rely on showy annuals.** Skip annuals altogether and plant long-term, sustainable perennials instead. If you *must* include annuals and are willing to replant them every single year, pretty please reserve them for seasonal window boxes and high-visibility containers.

- **Don't include too many different colors.** This is the easiest way to make a garden feel chaotic and lacking in a strong design sense. We *love* color, but even in a color-play garden style, select an edited color palette with a maximum of three main colors, and stick to it.

- **Don't choose too many different types of trees.** We give you a gold star for every new tree you plant in your small garden, but cap it at no more than two different species to keep the look cohesive.

- **Don't forget to mix your greens.** A garden with plants all in a similar shade of green and without contrasting lights and darks falls flat. Mix bright, lime green with deep, dark hunter green and silvery gray-green. P.S. The same goes for choosing plants with similar heights—but you will easily avoid this pitfall if you design high to low.

- **Don't select incompatible plants for the amount of sun.** You'll be tempted, but it's not worth a couple weeks of looking good for a lifetime of struggling to survive. Sun-dependent plants in the shade will get leggy and thin or even rot out. Shade-loving plants in the sun will burn, turn weird colors, guzzle water, or shrivel up and die (eek!).

TOP FIVE TREES

1. Wilson fruitless olive
   (*Olea europaea* 'Wilsonii')

2. Crape myrtle (*Lagerstroemia indica*)

3. 'Little Gem' magnolia (*Magnolia grandiflora* 'Little Gem')

4. Eastern or western redbud
   (*Cercis canadensis* 'Forest Pansy'
   or *Cercis occidentalis*)

5. Arabian lilac (*Vitex trifolia* 'Purpurea')

(See page 174 for more recommended trees.)

Highest: Start at the Top

The highest plants in the garden are the trees. In top-to-bottom plant design, always start with the trees. Decide how they need to work (function) first, then how they will look (form). A single, well-placed shade tree can take a pretty-to-look-at garden to a pretty-to-live-in garden.

TREES FOR THE SMALL GARDEN

Buy the biggest container tree by the gallon or box that you can afford and plant it first. This doesn't mean buy the biggest type of tree—remember the scale!—because a tree that is too big will take over your garden. In general, as the largest living element, trees elevate the mood and change the physical climate of a small garden.

Choose Your Trees

- The small garden can usually take a maximum of two different types of trees for a cohesive look.

- Choose a single large tree for high impact and broad shade canopy. The larger the tree, the farther to the edges and corners of the garden it should be planted.

- Repeat one type of small tree across your design.

- For potted trees, repeat the same type or family of tree.

- A small-focal-point tree can draw attention with blooms, trunk texture, leaf color, or intriguing habit, like a weeping mayten.

- If you need to keep your trees in containers, refer back to page 59 for a list of the best patio trees and "Instant Orchard" inspiration.

Work Your Trees

- Create a living focal point, such as this sunny yellow *Parkinsonia* 'Desert Museum' shown opposite.

- Shade a dining or sitting area with a natural ceiling canopy—and skip the pricey trellis!

- Anchor and soften house corners.

- Balance the height of the house by anchoring the opposite garden corner.

- Add height to a low planting bed.

- Screen the street or parking area with a single large tree.

- Line the entry path to make the front door the focal point.

- Provide year-round shade with evergreen trees.

- Plant deciduous trees for seasonally adjusting summer shade and bare-branch winter sun.

High: Set Your Backdrops and Screens

After your trees, set the stage to a beautiful small garden with high hedges, shrubs, and vines. Not every garden needs a vine, but they are the miracle workers of the small garden, adding wild, twisting mystery and movement.

DESIGN WITH VINES

If you're short on floor space but need broad coverage to screen a neighbor, green up a fence, or hide a wall, then vines are your new BFFs! Even if you don't need coverage, consider tossing in a vine. They're the welcome high-climbing wild card in the garden. Vines can grow in a planting space as small as 1 foot wide but are screening machines that can grow multitudes taller and wider without encroaching on your valuable floor space.

IDEAS AND TIPS FOR SELECTING VINES

- Choose vines for leaf coverage, color, bloom, and size depending on how they need to work in your garden.

- In a small garden, it's best to stick with one type of vine for a clean look.

- Your ultimate vine choice should relate to your garden style. A wild romantic look might call for layers of different rambling wisteria or lilac vines spilling into each other; a traditional garden might use Boston ivy (*Parthenocissus tricuspidata* 'Veitchii') to screen a wall; and a color garden might crave magenta or red bougainvilleas along a back fence.

- A single vine with a strong color, form, or bloom can make a great focal point.

- Most vines need a support structure, such as a fence, wall, trellis, or wire, but some varieties will be self-supporting over time.

- Plant any vine that attaches directly to your house wall, such as creeping fig (*Ficus pumila*), with caution because it will erode your structure over time.

- Keep a close watch on the vigorous vines and tip prune often to keep them from taking over.

TOP FIVE VINES

1. Royal trumpet vine (*Distictis* 'Rivers')
2. Flame vine (*Pyrostegia venusta*)
3. Cup of gold vine (*Solandra maxima*)
4. Hardy kiwi vine (*Actinidia arguta*)
5. Wisteria (*Wisteria*)

(See page 174 for more recommended vines.)

PERFUME WALL ▶

A single blooming vine such as the vanilla-scented *Distictis laxiflora* 'Vanilla Orchid' can make a stunning focal point when neatly trained onto a wall with wire.

PRIVACY PLEASE: TALL SHRUBS, HEDGES, AND SCREENING PLANTS

After you have selected your trees and vines, it's time to fill in with your tall shrubs and hedges. Look toward the perimeter of your garden to see where you need privacy or screening to make something disappear; or look for an area that could use a single tall plant as a showy focal point. Choose hedges that are low-maintenance and/or give you a flower or color that adds interest to your garden.

TOP FIVE TALL SHRUBS OR HEDGES

1. Pineapple guava (*Feijoa sellowiana*; opposite). A garden-to-table favorite for its tropical, edible blooms.

2. Texas privet (*Ligustrum japonica* 'Texanum'). Best green machine (with many other varieties for every climate) for its disease-resistant glossy green leaves and white spring blooms, and that it grows a perfect 8 to 12 feet with minimal pruning. If there were a Texas Privet Club, we would be the presidents.

3. Fern pine (*Podocarpus gracilior*). Lush and low-water, this plant has feathery, graceful leaves.

4. 'Moonlight' grevillea (*Grevillea* 'Moonlight'). An unexpected hedge choice that's also a hummingbird magnet—great for kids in a family garden.

5. Semidwarf citrus trees. Evergreen with a natural shrub form and ornamental edibles that smells good, looks good, and tastes good in recipes and cocktails.

(See page 175 for more recommended tall shrubs.)

FRUIT TREE HEDGES AND EDIBLE FLOWERS

Plant wisely, and you can have your cake and eat it, too! Hedges that produce fruit and edible flowers or leaves (such as blackberry, kumquat, and laurel/bay leaf) are a vibrant and often fragrant way to bring color and screening into an outdoor room. This pineapple guava (*Feijoa sellowiana*) hedge beats a fence, and the best part is their blooms make great garnishes. It's our favorite as it takes the cake (literally) for both pretty color and privacy.

Medium: Mid-Level Magic

Shrubs' magic lies in their ability to add garden texture, soften the house foundation, screen that old wood fence, and work as "walls" in an outdoor room.

MEDIUM EVERGREEN SHRUBS AND THE 80/20 RULE

Shrubs are the woody, bushy plants that branch from the ground and provide most of the plant structure and volume in a small garden. Evergreen shrubs retain their foliage and look good all year, while deciduous shrubs lose their leaves during the winter months and often return with a brilliant spring bloom. About 80 percent of the medium-level garden plants should be shrubs and the remaining 20 percent should be blooming perennials and grasses.

TOP FIVE MEDIUM EVERGREEN SHRUBS

1. Dwarf pittosporum (*Pittosporum crassifolium* 'Compactum')

2. Little Ollie (*Olea europaea* 'Montra')

3. Little river wattle (*Acacia cognata* 'Cousin Itt')

4. Dwarf yeddo hawthorn (*Rhaphiolepis umbellata* 'Minor')

5. Boxwood (*Buxus* 'Green Mountain')

(See page 176 for more recommended evergreen shrubs.)

MEDIUM FLOWERING PERENNIALS

Herbaceous (nonwoody) perennials are plants that live for many growing seasons (or indefinitely), but die back in the cooler months. Perennials often spread with time and improve in shape and bloom with fertilizer and water (even in the dormant months). It's a good idea to cut them back to ground level annually.

TOP FIVE MEDIUM FLOWERING PERENNIALS

1. Gray-leaved French lavender (*Lavandula dentata* var. *candicans*)

2. Mexican sage (*Salvia leucantha* 'Santa Barbara')

3. 'Blue Spire' Russian sage (*Perovskia atriplicifolia* 'Blue Spire')

4. Fern-leaf yarrow (*Achillea filipendulina*)

5. Tall verbena (*Verbena bonariensis*)

(See page 176 for more recommended perennials.)

PLANT RECIPE:
MODERN MONOCHROME SHRUB GARDEN ▶

Hedge: *Ligustrum japonicum* 'Texanum', **Evergreen shrubs:** *Rhaphiolepis umbellata* 'Minor', *Pittosporum crassifolium* 'Compactum', *Westringia fruticosa* 'Grey Box'. **Perennial:** *Phlomis* 'Grande Verde'.

DON'T FORGET YOUR GREENS!
Mix shades of greens—from
chartreuse bright to muted
grays to deep emerald—for
healthy contrast.

GRASSES

Ornamental grasses are also perennials, and many fall in the "medium" height category and add soft, flowy magic. Almost every garden can benefit from the texture and movement of ornamental grasses (or grasslike plants), and there's one for every condition from full sun to shade. Small grasses work great mixed with succulents, tucked into hardscape pockets, planted in between boulders and at the base of containers. Many grasslike plants stay lush all year and do not need to be cut back, such as dwarf mat rush, blue flax lily, and small cape rush.

Small Garden Grasses

A 'Canyon Prince' wild rye (*Leymus condensatus* 'Canyon Prince')

B Hare's tail (*Lagurus ovatus*)

C Oriental fountain grass (*Pennisetum orientale*)

D 'Karl Foerster' feather reed grass (*Calamagrostis × acutiflora* 'Karl Foerster')

E Small cape rush (*Elegia tectorum*)

F Berkeley sedge (*Carex divulsa*)

G Mexican feather grass (*Nassella tenuissima*) (Check local invasive list before planting)

H Blue flax lily (*Dianella caerulea* 'Cassa Blue')

I Autumn moor-grass (*Sesleria autumnalis*)

J Blue moor-grass (*Sesleria caerulea*)

K Dwarf mat rush (*Lomandra longifolia* 'Breeze')

L Dwarf mondo grass (*Ophiopogon japonicus* 'Nana')

M 'Elijah Blue' blue fescue (*Festuca glauca* 'Elijah Blue')

Low: Dig In

Low layers are just as big of a priority as the high, especially in the small-scale garden where every inch counts. It ensures you're not looking at dirt! Ground covers, pollinators, and small succulents give the base layer a low, lush visual impact.

After a full garden goes in, you're still staring at mostly dirt. Don't forget the ground cover: It's a finishing layer of very low-growing plants that can be just as gorgeous as the bigger plants and pulls the whole garden together. There are many options, so cover your dirt and have some fun.

Teeny Ground Covers

A Little ears (*Falkia repens*)

B Woolly thyme
(*Thymus praecox*)

C Elfin thyme
(*Thymus serpyllum* 'Elfin')

D 'Silver Falls' dichondra
(*Dichondra argentea*
'Silver Falls')

E Silver carpet
(*Dymondia margaretae*)

F Australian violet
(*Viola hederacea*)

The Birds and the Bees: Ground Covers for Pollinators

Instead of basic, familiar, green ground cover, why not choose an enticing bloom to attract hummingbirds, bees, and butterflies? If family members have bee allergies, skip the bee magnets and focus on butterfly friendly plants, such as yarrow (*Achillea*) instead. Flag down the fliers with these easy strategies:

- Include red and orange blooms with trumpet-shaped flowers to cue the hummingbirds.

- Plant blooms for every season.

- Incorporate herbs.

- Add native species.

- Add a shallow water feature with a landing spot, such as a boulder bird bath (see page 92) so that the hard-working pollinators stay hydrated.

- Avoid pesticide use.

SAVE THE BEES!

Bees especially love *Teucrium chamaedrys*, which works as an excellent pathway liner or clipped nosegay in small vases.

Pollinator Ground Covers

A Ground morning glory (*Convolvulus sabatius*)

B Creeping thyme (*Thymus serpyllum*)

C 'Walker's Low' catmint (*Nepeta racemosa* 'Walker's Low')

D Dwarf wall germander (*Teucrium chamaedrys* 'Nanum')

E Prostrate rosemary (*Rosmarinus officinalis* 'Lockwood de Forest')

F Sea thrift (*Armeria maritima*)

G Blue star creeper (*Isotoma fluviatilis*)

H 'Silver Falls' dichondra (*Dichondra argentea* 'Silver Falls')

I Common thyme (*Thymus vulgaris*)

CAN'T-LOSE MINI SUCCULENTS

If you're looking for succulents that are easy to love and hard to kill, then the echeveria variety are at the top of our list. These garden gems have a pretty rosette form and happily produce pups on their own. They can even be popped into spots with limited soil space. In cold-weather climates, keep succulents in containers that can be brought indoors or think of them as annuals that will need to be refreshed or replaced yearly—it's the one "annual" that we think is worth the trouble! Here's a peek at our top performing small succulents we can't live without.

Recipe-Tested Small Succulents

A Hens and chicks
(*Sempervivum* 'Blue Boy')

B Houseleek (*Sempervivum calcareum*)

C Common houseleek
(*Sempervivum tectorum*)

D Pink iceplant (*Oscularia deltoides*)

E Ghost echeveria (*Echeveria lilacina*)

F Blue chalksticks (*Senecio serpens*)

G *Echeveria cante*

H *Echeveria* 'Joan Daniel'

I Pork and beans (*Sedum rubrotinctum*)

J 'Angelina' stonecrop
(*Sedum rupestre* 'Angelina')

K *Echeveria colorata*

L *Echeveria* 'Perle von Nürnberg'

M 'Little Gem' stonecrop (*Sedum* × *cremnosedum* 'Little Gem')

N Narrow-leaf chalkstick (*Senecio talinoides* subsp. *cylindricus*)

O Mother-of-pearl plant
(*Graptopetalum paraguayense*)

P *Echeveria* 'Dark Prince' (*Echeveria agavoides* 'Dark Prince')

Q *Sedeveria* 'Green Rose'

R Donkey's tail (*Sedum morganianum*)

S Blue Spruce stonecrop (*Sedum rupestre* 'Blue Spruce')

T *Graptoveria* 'Fred Ives'

U Coppertone stonecrop (*Sedum nussbaumerianum*)

V String of beads (*Senecio rowelyanus*)

W Mexican gem (*Echeveria elegans*)

X Kiwi aeonium (*Aeonium haworthii* 'Kiwi')

Top-to-Bottom Plant Design Deconstructed ▶

This pied-à-terre shows all the elements of high-to-low plant design, from trees, vines, and hedges to shrubs, succulents, and ground covers. The design has strong repetition, layers of texture, a cohesive color palette, and a stunning plant focal point. Let's break it down high to low.

Highest

Tree: Jacaranda (*Jacaranda mimosifolia*), a stunning single tree that provides height and shade in violet tones.

High

Vine: Morning glory (*Ipomoea indica*) brings color onto the distant view when planted on the fence behind the hedge.

Hedge: Texas privet (*Ligustrum japonica* 'Texanum') creates a clean, green backdrop wall and privacy screen for this streetside garden.

High Focal Point: 'Marginata' century plant (*Agave americana* 'Marginata') rises up from the ground covers and its variegated yellow leaves contrast with the purple blooms, while the large solid form provides contrasting scale and texture.

Medium

Evergreen Shrub: Iceberg rose (*Rosa* 'Iceberg') has white blooms that give relief to all the purple and contrast against the deep greens of the garden.

Flowering Perennial: Chiapas sage (*Salvia chiapensis*), a medium-height perennial shrub, adds pink to the middle plane of the garden.

Grass: Dwarf mat rush (*Lomandra longifolia* 'Breeze') provides green texture around the tree base and thrives under its partly shaded canopy.

Low

Ground Covers: Rozanne geranium (*Geranium* 'Gerwat'), blue-green sedge (*Carex flacca*), lamb's ear (*Stachys byzantina* 'Helen von Stein'), and blue sedge (*Carex flacca* 'Blue Zinger') provide simple, repeated ground covers to create a full, textured, bloomy border with silvers and greens.

Aloes: Coral aloe (*Aloe striata*) adds solid leaf structure in the border and provides an unexpected winter coral-color bloom.

Design Tip: For nonstop seasonal color, the jacaranda tree starts the bloom train in spring, followed by roses and salvias in summer, trailed by geraniums and morning glories in fall, and finally, the coral aloe finishes strong with orange blooms in winter.

5

CONTAINER GARDENS

A container garden is an easy way to test all your new plant and design skills in one small spot to make a microgarden with maximum impact. Containers allow you to create a garden anywhere in any space, no matter how small. You don't even need dirt on the ground! Here are some of our favorite ways to work containers into a garden.

10 WAYS TO USE CONTAINERS IN THE SMALL GARDEN

1. Make an instant hedge, such as these Texas privet (*Ligustrum japonica* 'Texanum') hedges (opposite), by planting several in white fiber-reinforced cement containers.

2. Install an instant wall for safety along a drop-off.

3. Create an instant focal point (left) without waiting for a tree to grow or having to buy a new house with an ocean view.

4. Build a water fountain with a recirculating pump or a faux fountain with cascading plantings (see page 69).

5. Raise your style with a veggie garden in pretty pots and troughs.

6. Define an entryway with containers along a path to direct the eye forward.

7. Add a planted centerpiece to elevate an outdoor living room.

8. Soften hardscape and create coziness with clusters of containers full of textures.

9. Add an architectural element in a planted area that needs weight.

10. Show off your personal style with unique containers on your porch before your guests step inside.

▲ **Design Tip:** Spiky and soft create a complimentary yin and yang in the garden, like this *Agave potatorum* 'El Camarón' in a container nestled in a drift of billowy *Nassella tenuissima* grass.

Build a Container Garden, Step by Step

Just as you'd start planning for a small garden, building a container garden also begins with planning for function, location, and scale. Apply the same principles of *space* and *scale* to choose the size of the container and its location in the garden. Play with *eye candy, focal points,* and *repetition* in selecting contrasting, textural plants. We'll break this all down step by step so you can get the look you want in your yard, balcony, entryway, paved patio, or deck.

STEP 1: DECISION TIME

First off, ask yourself: What is the container's function? Where do you want to place your containers? How much space do you have (how big can you go?).

Here are a few jobs containers can do really well:

- Add architectural interest by providing a solid form in a mass of soft plants
- Fake a fountain (no water line, no electricity for a pump, no problem!)
- Provide focal points by capturing the gaze and directing the eye around the garden
- Grow easy veggies, herbs, and flowers in raised planters
- Create a welcome area (fluff your porch, show off your style), see page 154
- Define a space with planter walls when the hardscape can't be changed
- Soften up the hardscape (no sledge hammer required)

After you've figured out the function, look around and decide where the container will live to select the right size container and plants that will thrive long-term.

- How many hours of direct or indirect sun will the container receive? Spend some time outside and notice how the sun moves across your garden before you pick your plants.
- Is it south-facing (hottest) or north-facing (shadiest)? South-facing plants need to be extra tough to withstand direct sun for many hours a day. North-facing plants can be more delicate and are often in danger of rot if they are overwatered in the container.
- Can you add an automatic drip irrigation tube or will it need hand-watering? If you don't install irrigation, you get the job! If you can't hide or connect an automatic drip tube, then select drought-resistant plants that need less attention.
- What's the setting? Look at surrounding plantings and structures to coordinate and contrast plant color and textures.

Next you will need to determine what is the best scale and size for the space. Here are some designer tips to get started.

- Measure your space. Draw an outline for the container footprint in chalk or painter's tape and write down the measurements before you purchase.

- Define your scale. Containers should not generally be taller than furniture in the same zone, and front porch containers shouldn't hide outdoor sconces or address numbers. Focal point containers can be bigger and taller than others in the garden.

- Decide if you want a single container or a grouping of containers. In asymmetrical gardens, one and three are the magic numbers. Two matching containers make a winning symmetrical layout.

BIGGER IS BETTER! ▶

Just as with trees, buy the biggest container you can afford that is appropriate for the space you have. Fewer and bigger is almost always more dramatic than more and smaller. Good to know: A container with a 30-inch-wide opening is a great statement that looks big at the nursery, looks even bigger at home, and will keep its impact filled with plants.

STEP 2:
FIND YOUR STYLE AND MATERIAL

You've put so much thought into designing your garden, the container will take your style to the finish line. The container is to the garden as the shoe is to the dress—it makes the outfit! The shape, detail, and material are ways to accessorize your personal style. For example, take traditional terra-cotta clay pots into a modern realm by choosing ones with square lips or rectangular shapes. Move indoor baskets onto outdoor porches or repurpose metal corrugated bins into garden vessels (make sure to add liners and drainage holes). In general, larger plants and patio trees need more root space, thus larger containers. But have fun mixing and matching your styles and materials.

Traditional

TRADITIONAL

Pedestals and containers with rounded and rolled lips or square containers with texture detail can also lean formal. Go-to materials include terra-cotta clay, gray stone, zinc, and iron. Works with Old World and New Traditional garden styles.

REPURPOSED

Channel vintage, rustic, or cottage looks with French flower buckets, baskets, jars, crocks, galvanized tins, and pedestal urns in metal, ceramic, rattan, and wood. Works with Organic Modern, Global Boho, and Urban Homestead garden styles.

TRANSITIONAL

Bridge traditional and modern by using timeless materials with contemporary shapes—a glazed ceramic container with a geometric pattern or a pedestal planter in concrete. Works with Color Play, Urban Homestead, and really every garden style!

MODERN

Smooth textures and simple shapes with square lips lean modern. Always modern materials include concrete, fiber-reinforced concrete (that looks like stone), and uniform ceramic glazes in whites and grays. Works with Clean Minimalist and Bold Eclectic garden styles.

Repurposed

Transitional

Modern

STEP 3: CHOOSE A SINGLE CONTAINER OR A TRIO

Choose one single container to stand on its own or three containers to work together depending on your space, style, and the container's purpose. If you have the room, a cluster of three planters always commands attention on front porches, in a row of veggie beds, or set on the corner of a patio. Single containers work best as focal points and to add architectural interest in the garden.

SINGLE LADY

One container will draw attention to itself so the planter and its plants should either be big, interesting, or wild. This little square concrete container pictured at left fits perfectly in the window cutout with a tumbledown wax plant (*Hoya carnosa*). Even though it's not big, it's wild and interesting against the negative space of the white wall background.

THREE AMIGOS

Three snuggled containers win every time if you have the space. Choose similar container colors and materials and vary heights in tall, medium, and low. If you choose all the same material, mix up the shapes of the containers. Provide contrast with a different shape plant in each container. Pictured opposite, the forms are solid rosette, upright fountain, and cascading and lacy. To keep this look modern and minimal, the color palette is limited to shades of green.

PLANT RECIPE: MODERN WHITE AND GREEN ▶

Left to right: *Asplenium nidus, Aeonium canariense, Acacia cognata* 'Cousin Itt'.

STEP 4: PICK YOUR PLANTS

The tight planting space in a container means that every plant matters and should be chosen first for its form, habit, and color—with contrast and texture at the forefront. Form is the shape (column, sphere, fan) of the plant and habit is how it grows (twisting, arching, creeping). It's good to have a plant list before you shop, *but* if you know the container planting space you have, you can go to the nursery (untethered!) and select plants for contrast without a specific list. Ask the nursery manager to describe the plant size and habit in its mature form since young plants often look different from their adult selves—just like us!

GOOD FORM

Knowing your plant forms and how to combine them means that you can shop locally for plant varieties that thrive in your region without actually knowing the plant names (but you get extra credit if you can say them, too). Just like shopping for shoes, you might look for a wedge or slide or sneaker to go with your outfit before you flip over the shoe and see the specific brand name (or price tag). Start thinking in form and shape, and you'll be designing on the fly in no time.

 **EFFORTLESS ECLECTIC**

Mix finishes, sizes, and shapes of containers but keep the eclectic look cohesive with a tight green color palette for the plants (*Rhipsalis baccifera*, *Olea europaea* 'Montra', *Sedum morganianum*, *Asparagus densiflorus* 'Myers'). In cooler climates, a boxwood (*Buxus*) could be paired with creeping Jenny (*Lysimachia nummularia*) for a similar (but winterproof) look.

A Few Forms and Habits to Know

A Branched and open

B Upright and vining

C Delicate and spreading

D Rosette and round

E Bushy and full

F Fountain and arching

G Trunked and sculptural

H Cascading and spilling

For plant suggestions by form, see page 177. Now that you know all your plant forms, on the following pages you'll find a couple tried and true approaches to creating stylish containers using contrast.

THRILL, FILL, AND SPILL

This catchy rule (which we didn't invent; it's a longtime garden legend) for combining container plants works best for larger containers. Bring the *thrill* with upright, columnar, trunked, and fountain forms. Add the *fill* with bushy, delicate, and rosette forms. Finish the *spill* with cascading and spilling forms. The spillers usually get longer and more impressive as they mature. But for smaller gardens and containers, the Thrill, Fill, and Spill rule is often just too many plants. A better system is one we call "The Perfect Power Couple."

THE PERFECT POWER COUPLE

Let's face it. Three can be a crowd. Our containers (which trend modern and minimal) rarely have visual or practical space to arrange three different types of plants in one container. Photographing fourteen different Isa Bird gardens and oodles of containers for this book proved that our signature container plant design is the "Power Couple." Trim down the Thrill, Fill, and Spill formula to just two selections with contrasting plant forms—a columnar with a spreading, a bushy with a spilling, a sculptural with a delicate—and you will become a mix-and-match master.

▶ **PLANT RECIPE: POWER COUPLE**

Thrill: *Echeveria lilacina.*
Fill: *Sedum rupestre 'Blue Spruce'.*

◀ **PLANT RECIPE: THRILL, FILL, AND SPILL**

Thrill: *Elegia tectorum.*
Fill: *Graptopetalum paraguayense.*
Spill: *Sedum rowleyanus.*

◄ Citrus Container Garden Deconstructed

A vibrant focal point and colorful container doubles as a stylish citrus garden.

- This patio tree's function is to work as a focal point and it's doing an A+ job.

- The scale of the dwarf tree is just right, adding height but not so big as to overwhelm the other plants in the container.

- Brights are carried from orange kumquat to purple succulent to the turquoise container, making it perfect for the Color Play garden (see page 50).

- The plant recipe includes a "thriller," dwarf kumquat tree (*Fortunella margarita* 'Nagami'); "filler," *Echeveria elegans* and *Echeveria* 'Perle von Nürnberg'; and "spiller," textural pink iceplant (*Oscularia deltoides*).

◄ **Design Tip:** Underplant citrus trees with a bed of succulents for graphic, layered patio containers. The small root-balls of most succulents make them perfect for understory plants that avoid root competition with the shallow spreading roots of citrus.

Rethink the Veggie Bed

Herbs, fruits, vegetables, and edible flowers are wonderful additions to the small garden and can be as ornamental as they are practical. Reconsider the veggie container itself beyond a functional vessel for growing food and rather as an integral, cheerful design element for your garden. The material can vary from wood to ceramic to concrete to steel; in other words, a veggie "box" doesn't need to look like a box. Reframe the veggie garden as a focal point; a solid architectural shape that adds weight and balance; a way to reinforce the garden style; or a conversation piece.

TIPS FOR VEGGIE CONTAINERS

- Ensure excellent drainage with ample drainage holes.
- If placing containers directly on the ground, remove the bottom, which allows the roots to grow deeper.
- Add gopher wire along the bottom to protect your veggies from burrowing animals.
- Add automatic drip irrigation tubing through the bottom of the container whenever possible, to make watering a breeze and to avoid unsightly tubes snaking up the sides of your pots.
- Buy organic vegetable garden soil to ensure good drainage and healthy plants—it's worth every penny!
- Allow the soil to dry between waterings and adjust with the weather.
- Use organic slug/snail bait as needed.
- Don't forget to harvest your veggies!

WHAT TO GROW

1. Cherry tomatoes and mini veggies: Nantes carrot, radish, Sungold cherry tomato
2. Herbs and edible flowers: Mixed oreganos, thymes, basils, chives, cilantro, nasturtiums, pansies
3. Leafy greens: Bright Lights Swiss chard, Red Russian kale, dino kale, mixed lettuces
4. Small climbers: Lemon cucumber, bush beans, Japanese eggplant
5. Small fruit trees: Semidwarf varieties of 'Meyer' lemon, makrut lime, Mexican lime, caviar lime, kumquat, satsuma mandarin, Mission and Negronne fig, fruiting olive

BEYOND THE BOX: STYLE GUIDE FOR VEGGIE, HERB + EDIBLE FLOWER CONTAINERS

Think outside the generic redwood box! As with all design elements in the small garden, the veggie garden is a prominent feature and presents a unique opportunity to do something different. Match your container to your style and make your edible garden a statement piece in your outdoor space. Integrate edible flowers into every container for good looks and interesting garnishes.

Container Materials

A   Galvanized trough + African marigolds

B   Terra-cotta + strawberries and basil

C   Terra-cotta flower bucket + Indio Mandarinquat (a cross between a mandarin orange and a kumquat makes a mind-blowing mini-orange)

D   Powder-coated trough + dark opal basil with yellow pear tomatoes

◀ COOL CONCRETE

A square concrete planter makes a modern ornamental herb garden when filled with chives that bloom as the plants mature.

Edible Flowers

Up your garnish game by adding colorful edible flowers and a few spicy leaves to salads, cheese plates, cakes, cookies, and cocktails.

A Pomegranate flower

B Purple pansy

C English lavender

D Marigold

E Blue African basil blossom

F Pink zinnia

G Chive blossom

H Pineapple guava

I Variegated nasturtium leaf

J Johnny-Jump-Up viola

K English thyme

L Purple basil

GARDEN TO BAR

Shake up an ounce of vodka with fresh
squeezed lemon and lime juices. Pour over
ice with a splash of soda and garnish with
makrut lime, cilantro blossom, lavender,
blackberry, and mint. Cheers!

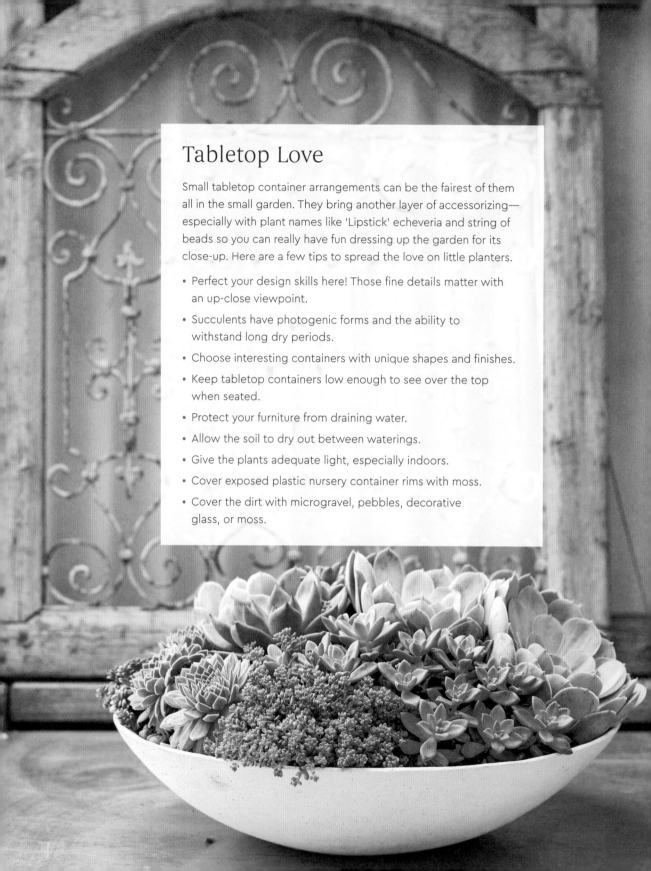

Tabletop Love

Small tabletop container arrangements can be the fairest of them all in the small garden. They bring another layer of accessorizing—especially with plant names like 'Lipstick' echeveria and string of beads so you can really have fun dressing up the garden for its close-up. Here are a few tips to spread the love on little planters.

- Perfect your design skills here! Those fine details matter with an up-close viewpoint.
- Succulents have photogenic forms and the ability to withstand long dry periods.
- Choose interesting containers with unique shapes and finishes.
- Keep tabletop containers low enough to see over the top when seated.
- Protect your furniture from draining water.
- Allow the soil to dry out between waterings.
- Give the plants adequate light, especially indoors.
- Cover exposed plastic nursery container rims with moss.
- Cover the dirt with microgravel, pebbles, decorative glass, or moss.

PLANT RECIPE: TABLETOP TERRA-COTTA HEART

Echeveria 'Black Prince', *Echeveria minima, Graptopetalum amethystinum*

Front Door Fix

If you've got the space, let it shine. A porch is the best place to create a front door greeting for your guests. A trio of matching modern terra-cotta containers in three different heights is our power of three. The plants provide a cheerful hello along with a welcome mat and chalkboard greeting sign.

QUICK FIX IDEAS

- Fresh front door paint and vibrant plant colors
- A peek of purple adds a wild card
- Large planters close to the front door to fill empty porch space
- Graphic house numbers
- Welcome sign in planter and playful doormat
- Modern sconce

CREATE A BOLD FOCAL POINT

Small entries often have imperfections (chipped tile and stone, peeling paint on a rental) or nondecorative elements (power boxes, pipes, outlets, gas meters), which are eyesores. Hide unsightly items with an oversized planter that transforms into a focal point and looks as hip as the home dwellers inside.

Staying Alive!
How Not to Kill Your Container Plants

Here are our top tips for making sure your container plants survive, thrive, and stay aliiiiive. Legend says if you talk or sing to your plants they'll grow better. You tell us!

- Choose your plants to match the light conditions of your container.

- Match your soil to your plants—always go organic and match cacti mix to succulents, organic veggie blend to vegetables, and organic potting soil blend for everything else.

- Plant high, within 1 inch of the container rim, because your plants will settle over time with watering.

- Fertilize on a regular schedule, one to three times per year with liquid slow-release fertilizer depending on the plants' needs.

- Ensure adequate drainage holes in the bottom of the containers. Don't even think about planting in a container without drainage holes. If they aren't included, then grab a drill and make em!

- Set your containers on tiles or terra-cotta feet to encourage good drainage. Saucers help prevent water stains on your patio, but they are one of the top causes of root rot when containers sit in water. Our advice is to skip the saucers for a clean, less cluttered look.

- Fill the entire container with potting soil. We do not advise filling the bottom of the container with styrofoam, which can make the container dangerously top-heavy.

- Water on a regular schedule depending on your plant, and let the soil dry in between watering.

- Avoid planting poisonous or thorny plants by high traffic areas. Your friends and family will thank you.

6

DESIGNER TOOL KIT

Think of this tool kit like your ultimate primer. Just like you'd use paint primer and prep your walls before painting or read a recipe before cooking, you want to run through these tools before planning and planting your garden. Just as that layer of primer rewards you with a spectacular paint finish or prepping a five-course dinner the night before guarantees a smooth party, our designer tool kit will set you and your garden up for success.

Assess Your Space

It may sound obvious, but when designing your small garden, start with the space you have. We call it a reality check. You (like us) may have always dreamt of having an infinity lap pool, but let's look to see if there is even a space for a soaking tub. You might love bright blooming salvias and sunflowers for a summer cottage garden style, but let's make sure your space receives enough sun each day to produce those flowers. Lastly, let's look at what we love and what we don't and perhaps what we need to hide stat.

Go outside to your garden space and jot down answers to the following questions. Then take a bunch of photos from every angle. Print and post on your wall, or make a nifty collage with the images on your computer. Assess your space again looking at the photos. This might help you look at it in a newer unbiased way.

- What's your first impression? How does the space make you feel?
- What are the setting, location, and light in the morning, midday, and late afternoon?
- What are the strengths of your space (a pretty view, a nice window, French doors, shaded patio, friendly neighbor)?
- What are the challenges (slope, exposed space, awkward layout, unclear entry, traffic noise, unsightly fence, utility box, bedroom window, lack of privacy)?
- Where do you need focal points?
- What elements need screening for privacy and which areas need enclosure to create more coziness?

Map Your Space

One of the benefits of a small garden is that you can easily measure and diagram your space and make a base plan (scale map of your existing house footprint, property lines, and landscape features) with a few simple tools. Grab a tape measure, 25-foot or longer (30-foot is our sweet-spot); grid paper and pencil; and sunscreen and hat (always!).

MEASURE YOUR SPACE AND MAKE A ROUGH DRAWING

Take all the measurements of your outdoor garden space and jot the numbers and rough outline of your house on blank paper. This drawing will be lopsided and will *not* be to scale (or look pretty enough to include in a book). This step is purely informational, not artistic—no need to be a Monet here. So grab a friend to hold one end of the tape measure or stick a screwdriver through the end to anchor the tape in place. Then on your drawing:

- Mark the footprint of your space or house edge that will border your garden on paper.

- Mark your doors and windows and how high your windows are. These measurements might be important later to help keep the kitchen window plantings low, add a focal point tree in the middle of your living room window, or plant ample screening by the bathroom window so your mom doesn't have to wear her bathing suit in the shower when she visits.

- Mark your property lines.

- Mark any hardscape elements that can't be moved or changed (patios, decks, stairs, fences).

- Add any landscape features that need to stay (large trees, hedges, planter beds, or that hot tub you couldn't sell on Craigslist) and their size and distance from your house or property line.

CHOOSE YOUR SCALE

Choose your "scale" on your grid paper, or what the real life distance is for each square on your grid. Grid paper comes in a variety of sizes; if you are borrowing your child's school grid paper with larger squares, the easiest scale is one graph square equals 1 foot. For smaller grids you can scale up, to make four squares equal 1 foot, and so on. There are also free online tools to print grid paper in different scales (10 squares = 1 foot ($\frac{1}{10}$ scale), 8 squares = 1 foot ($\frac{1}{8}$ scale), etc.)

DRAW YOUR BASE PLAN

Using the measurements from the rough outline of your space, redraw your house, property lines, and landscape features onto the graph paper at your chosen scale. The grid lines will show you where to stop and start each element of your base plan. Mark north-south-east-west on your plan (use an online map for help if you are lost in the city wilderness) and think about the sun's aspect, how it moves over your space. Note the north-facing shade spots and open south-facing sun.

ADD HARDSCAPE:
ON PAPER OR ON SITE

There are two ways to do this—the choice is yours. Either sketch on paper using your base plan—this is what the pros do; or take the boots-on-the-ground approach and mark your plan directly on site. We'll cover both methods, but first, here are some hardscape layout rules of thumb:

- Entry paths and other high-traffic pathways should be a minimum of 4 feet across.
- Low-traffic pathways should be a minimum of 30 inches.
- Choose your dining table for your family size and the number of guests you regularly entertain. If you have larger gatherings, think about overflow spaces where you can set up a folding table so you don't end up with a banquet size outdoor table for a family of four.
- Allow for a minimum of 3 feet around your dining table for chairs and traffic flow.
- Furniture should be placed 18 inches away from a fire pit or coffee table.
- A bistro patio with a small table and two chairs could be as small as 7 to 8 feet across.

- Plan on a minimum of 12 to 14 feet across for a dining patio.
- Round dining tables are space-efficient. A 48-inch round table can seat six to eight people and requires as little as 10 feet of patio area (12 to 14 feet is more comfortable).
- A cozy patio for four lounge chairs and a coffee table could be 10 feet by 12 feet.

SKETCH ON PAPER

Sketch out your new design using your simple base plan. Tape a clean piece of tracing paper over your base plan to build a layered design. Use the same scale you choose for the base plan (one square = 1 foot, four squares = 1 foot, and so on). Depending on your style, decide if you want a modern geometric layout, natural curves, or a combination of curves and rectangles. Draw the rough outlines of your outdoor rooms, paying attention to the grid scale. If this causes a moment of stress, do a couple jumping jacks or a sun salutation to loosen up. You will use multiple sheets of tracing paper and won't get your layout right on the first try.

Next, connect the rooms with pathways or stepping stones. If your property is sloped, note areas with grade changes. Lastly, add focal points and other hardscape features, such as fire pits, boulders, and birdbaths. Label the materials of each element on the hardscape plan (gravel, concrete paver, and so on). Add color for extra credit.

MARK ON SITE

If measuring and sketching your plan on paper sounds too daunting, we get it. You can lay out your ideas for patios, pathways, and furniture directly on the ground. If you've sketched it out (or even if not), you can try a few other easy ways to see how the elements fit in your space. Here are some tricks that are fast and painless.

SPRAY PAINT

For marking areas on dirt, water-based landscape spray paint from the hardware store works best. It's available in shocking fluorescent colors and is a go-to tool for landscape designers and contractors. Wet the dirt first to get the cleanest lines and erase areas with the toe of your boot. Even though it advertises itself as "washable," it requires a good hard scrub to remove, so don't spray it on anything too precious.

FLOUR DUST

Skip the trip to the store and get a bag of flour from the pantry. Using a measuring cup, scatter your lines in place and hose them down to start over. Fearless flour dusting will have you cooking up your outdoor dream room in no time.

LANDSCAPE FLAGS

Flags are a great tool to mark more precisely measured lines on site (or if your handmade lines are looking wild). Use your tape measure and flag the corners and edges of your landscape features first. Then connect the dots with spray or flour and you will see your hardscape plan come to life.

PLANT LAYOUT: ON PAPER OR ON SITE

You've defined your style and assessed your needs and space. You've drawn a base plan, created a hardscape plan, and chosen your plant palette in chapter 4. Yay! The legwork is done and now it's time to bring it all together with a plant layout and shopping list. Just like planning out the hardscape, here are two approaches to creating your planting plan. Either sketch your plants onto your hardscape plan (or onto your base plan if your hardscape is all set) or flag the plants directly on site for the hands-on crowd. Before explaining the two options, here are some design principles to remember:

- Plant your trees first, then place tall plants in the back, medium in the middle, and low in the front.
- Group plants with similar light and water needs.
- Groups plants together to create plant massings, as they occur in nature.
- Arrange your plants so that they're spaced at 80 percent of their full size. We all want an instant garden, but insta-pretty will quickly turn to insta-nightmare with plants that are overgrown, crowded, and hard to maintain. You will thank us later.
- Repetition is key. Plant a mass of this and then a mass of that and then go back to a mass of this.
- Odd man in. Plants want to be grouped with their family, or they want to shine on their own. Plant 80 to 90 percent of your plants in groups of threes, fives, and sevens.
- For feature plants, group in threes; for focal points, a single will do.

- Edit. Always check to see what you can simplify or spice up (remove or add).
- Plant for all seasons. Winter is often overlooked, but it can be a stunning time of year in the garden when most plants are dormant. Evergreens and shrubs with berries in cold climates and winter-blooming aloes in warm climates are fantastic additions to the small garden.

SKETCH YOUR PLANT MASSINGS

- Lay a piece of tracing paper over your hardscape plan. (If you didn't make a hardscape plan, proceed to option two: flag your plants, page 166.)
- First make an X where you want to plant your trees.
- Draw a loose circle around each grouping of high, medium, and low plants.
- Add a star for your focal point plants.
- Shade or color each bubble group for an easy plant massing key.
- Print your plant palette list and plant photo collage for reference and add the mature width of each plant. There are abundant online plant guides that include plant size and spacing suggestions.
- Use a plastic circle template (the kind used by art, drafting, and math students) at the same scale as your hardscape layout. If 1 inch = 1 foot on your graph paper hardscape plan, then a 3-inch diameter circle = 3-foot wide plant on your planting plan.
- First circle the canopy of your trees to see where they will cast shade.
- Draw each plant at the correct size in your high-medium-low plant grouping layout.
- Count your plants in each category and make a shopping list.

ALTERNATIVELY, FLAG YOUR PLANTS

- Print your plant palette list and plant photo collage for reference, then add the mature width of each plant. There are abundant online plant guides that include plant size and spacing suggestions.

- Grab a handful of landscape flags in at least five colors to flag the locations for your plants directly on site.

- Designate one color flag for each type of plant (i.e. green = tree, blue = grasses, and pink = agave) on your list and flag your layout starting from high to low.

- Work in one area of the garden at a time, moving high to low, trees to ground covers.

- Use a tape measure and start placing the "plants" (flags) in the ground at the correct spacing. Your garden will start to appear before your eyes and you can adjust spacing, add ground cover, and add or subtract plants just by moving the flags around.

- When you are satisfied with the layout, snap a photo to capture the layout for later.

- Count your "plants" (colored flags) in each category and make a shopping list.

WHEN TO DIY OR HIRE OUT

Always get at least two bids for your landscape project. Then, set a budget and get realistic about your skill and time. Many installers will be happy to help you divide up the project into the pieces that need a pro and the parts that are DIY-friendly.

DIY

Creating gravel patios and pathways

Installing wood or steel bender board for pathway edges (skip the plastic)

Laying prefab concrete pavers

Arranging pre-cut stone stepping-stones

Amending soil and planting

Spreading mulch

Placing small boulders

Converting a planter into a water garden

MAYBE DIY

Laying tile (hire a pro unless you are really that good)

Laying brick in sand

Connecting *low*-voltage landscape lighting

Installing a drip irrigation system

Building wood decks and stairs

Building wood fences

Setting natural boulder stairs (DIY weight-lifting anyone?)

HIRE A PRO

Laying tile

Pouring custom concrete

Laying stone or brick on a concrete slab

Installing transformers, high-voltage electrical, and gas lines for fire pits

Building stone walls (even dry-stacked walls are worth a professional mason)

Custom-cutting flagstone

Chiseling a custom boulder birdbath

The Nitty Gritty on Prep, Care, and Feeding

Dirt First! We cannot emphasize enough how important it is to properly prep your soil with the necessary, vital "amendments" (compost for sandy soil, sand for clay soil, and so on). If you are unsure of your soil needs, take a bucket of dirt to the nursery for evaluation. Or contact your local professional garden supplier to request a soils lab test that can reveal the exact soil makeup and nutrients present or missing. This is usually unnecessary unless your garden has a long history of sad-looking, discolored plants that fail to thrive despite your best efforts to water and fertilize. Your plants will be as healthy as the soil they are planted in.

- Organic Fertilizer: Include a slow-release granular or liquid organic fertilizer with your new plants to give them a boost; then fertilize on a regular schedule.

- Irrigation: Automatic irrigation using drip or microsprayers is preferred for water conservation (and not killing your plants while you are on vacation). New plants will need more water in the first year to get established.

- Maintenance: Whether you hire out or DIY, gardens (especially new gardens) need regular attention, such as regular pruning and weeding, to make sure they grow in as intended. Low maintenance does not mean no maintenance.

Landscape Lingo: Talk Like a Pro, Think Like a Pro

Learning a few landscape-specific terms will help you communicate better with your local nursery and gardener, get quotes, and order the correct plants. We will spare you our early mistake of ordering a whole row of hedges by their common name, Catalina cherry, which was misread as Carolina cherry, a totally different plant that didn't grow an inch in five years of dry shade. So trust us, a little landscape lingo does the garden good.

Annuals: "Disposable" flowering plants that bloom for a single season and need to be replanted each year.

Deadheading: Pruning faded blooms to encourage a longer blooming seasoning.

Deciduous: Shrubs and trees that lose their leaves each year.

Drainage: Diverting water away from your home. This is crucial to protect your structures in the wet season. When in doubt, consult a professional.

Drought-tolerant: Sustainable plant choices that don't require a lot of water. But even low-water plants require some water—only desert-style "xeriscape" plantings require zero irrigation.

Egress view: The important view as you exit your front door or look out your window. Design for both views, not just for curb appeal.

Evergreen: "Forever-green" plants that keep their leaves and needles all year.

Focal point: An element that attracts the viewer's eye.

Ground cover: Low-growing plants that spread over bare soil. Using ground covers is one of the easiest ways to make the garden feel finished and "designed."

Hardscape: All the nonliving features in the garden, such as pathways, stepping stones, patios, decks, wall, fences, fire pits, and fountains.

Mulch: Shredded bark (organic) or pebbles (inorganic) used to cover exposed dirt. Mulch makes a garden feel clean, finished, and camera-ready.

Perennials: Plants that bloom year after year.

Pup: A young offshoot of a plant that breaks away with roots attached for easy transplanting to "propagate" new plants.

Scientific plant names: Each plant has a Latin name that's crucial to know to ensure accurate orders. The more you start to say them, the more they start to roll off your tongue.

Seasonality: The season in which a plant blooms or looks its best. A well-rounded garden doesn't spend its whole bloomy paycheck during spring or summer.

Setback: The legal distance from the road, sidewalk, or property line where you can start building walls and structures.

Shrub: A multistem woody plant (smaller than a tree and bigger than a breadbox) that is often the overlooked workhorse of the garden.

Tip pruning: Removing the tips (usually 1 to 3 inches) of branches with hand clippers to encourage new growth, desired shape, and fullness.

Underplant: The practice of putting smaller plants close the base of a larger plant to hide a trunk or leggy stem.

Water feature: Any element containing water, such as a fountain, birdbath, trough, or simple bowl.

Top Plant Picks

It is both exciting and overwhelming to know that there are thousands of different nursery plants available to the home gardener. Over the years, we have tested many hundreds of varieties in Isa Bird gardens and find ourselves returning to some tried-and-true plants—the ones that look best over time and that fill our design toolbox with the colors, textures, and forms we need to create winning spaces. Here are a few of our top picks in each plant category, and we encourage you to use our list as a baseline to find similar-looking plants that will thrive in your region and in the conditions of your garden.

Small Trees We Love

LEAF COLOR

Arabian lilac (*Vitex trifolia* 'Purpurea'): purple, evergreen

'Bloodgood' Japanese maple (*Acer palmatum* 'Bloodgood'): red, deciduous

'Forest Pansy' redbud (*Cercis canadensis* 'Forest Pansy'): burgundy, deciduous

Japanese persimmon (*Diospyros kaki* 'Fuyu'): orange/yellow foliage and fruit, deciduous

Pearl acacia (*Acacia podalyriifolia*): silver, evergreen

Pomegranate (*Punica granatum*): orange/yellow foliage, red fruit, deciduous

Smoke tree (*Cotinus coggygria*): plum, deciduous

BARK AND BLOOM

Crape myrtle (*Lagerstroemia indica*): white and pink bloom, deciduous

Western redbud (*Cercis occidentalis*): pink bloom, deciduous

Gold medallion tree (*Cassia leptophylla*): yellow bloom, deciduous

Jack flowering pear (*Pyrus calleryana* 'Jaczam'): white bloom, deciduous

'Little Gem' magnolia (*Magnolia grandiflora* 'Little Gem'): large white bloom, evergreen

'Miss Satomi' kousa (*Cornus kousa* 'Miss Satomi'): pink bloom, deciduous

Parkinsonia (*Parkinsonia* 'Desert Museum'): chartreuse bark, yellow bloom, semideciduous

Strawberry tree (*Arbutus* 'Marina'): smooth rust bark, evergreen

SHAPE, FORM, AND FRUIT

Blue Atlas cedar (*Cedrus atlantica* 'Glauca Pendula'): blue, weeping, evergreen

Blue fan palm (*Brahea armata*): silver fan frond, evergreen

Citrus ('Meyer' lemon, Mexican lime, kumquat) (*Citrus*): ornamental fruit, evergreen

Frangipani (*Plumeria*): thick, open-branched; white, pink, and orange fragrant blooms; deciduous

Mayten (*Maytenus boaria*): light green, weeping, evergreen

Mission fig and Negronne fig (*Ficus carica* 'Mission' and *Ficus carica* 'Negronne'): open-branched, deciduous

'Swan Hill' fruitless olive (*Olea europaea* 'Swan Hill'): gray green, evergreen

Weeping European larch (*Larix decidua pendula*): green to yellow, weeping, deciduous

Divine Vines

BLOOMING

Bougainvillea (*Bougainvillea*): the purple, pink, red, orange, and white "flowers" are technically leaves but look and feel 100 percent flowery

'Cécile Brünner' climbing rose (*Rosa* 'Cécile Brünner'): fragrant, miniature light pink blooms

Chinese wisteria (*Wisteria sinensis*): romantic purple spring blooms

Clematis (*Clematis*): delicate vines with blooms in every color

Cup of gold vine (*Solandra maxima*): golden flowers the size of grapefruit

'Eden' climbing rose (*Rosa* 'Eden'): old-fashioned, double petal pink blooms

Flame vine (*Pyrostegia venusta*): outrageous orange fall color

Giant Burmese honeysuckle (*Lonicera hildebrandiana*): giant white and yellow, fragrant blooms

Purple lilac vine (*Hardenbergia violacea* 'Canoelands'): dripping purple blooms that last for months

Royal trumpet vine (*Distictis* 'Rivers'): purple-mauve trumpet-shaped flowers

'Sally Holmes' climbing rose (*Rosa* 'Sally Holmes'): large, single petal white blooms

Star jasmine (*Trachelospermum jasminoides*): sun, shade, wet, dry, this vine thrives in almost every condition with perfumed white blooms spring through fall

Vanilla trumpet vine (*Distictis laxiflora* 'Vanilla Orchid'): purple blooms that smell of vanilla

FOLIAGE

Boston ivy (*Parthenocissus tricuspidata* 'Veitchii'): green in summer and classic red/orange/yellow fall colors

Chocolate vine (*Akebia quinata*): delicate leaves and clusters of wine-colored blooms

Common hops (*Humulus lupulus*): fast-growing vine with ornamental green leaves and clusters of small white "cones" that turn golden in fall.

Creeping fig (*Ficus pumila*): small green vine that attaches directly to structures (caution!)

Grape vine (*Vitis vinifera*): long-lasting woody vine with ornamental leaves and fruit

Hardy kiwi (*Actinidia arguta*): Gorgeous large heart-shaped, green leaves and smooth, green fruit with architectural twisted stems that shine in the winter when the vine loses its leaves. Necessary to plant a male *and* female plant less than 50 feet apart

BEST PATTERN-MAKERS (ESPALIER TREES AND VINES)

Azalea (*Rhododendron*): deciduous

Camellia (*Camellia*): evergreen

Fruit trees and vines (fig, apple, pear, grape): deciduous

Lavender star flower (*Grewia occidentalis*): evergreen

'Meyer' lemon (*Citrus × limon* 'Meyer') or 'Eureka' lemon (*Citrus × limon* 'Eureka'): or most citrus, evergreen

Pink powderpuff (*Calliandra haematocephala*): evergreen

Star jasmine (*Trachelospermum jasminoides*): evergreen

Best Bet Tall Shrubs, Hedges, and Screening Plants

BULLETPROOF GREEN SCREENS

Bright 'n' Tight Carolina laurel (*Prunus caroliniana* 'Monus'): Easily controlled, with dense, dark foliage

Fern pine (*Podocarpus gracilior*): wonderful fernlike foliage and great for tall screening

Texas privet (*Ligustrum japonica* 'Texanum'): disease-resistant glossy green leaves, white spring bloom, and grows 8 to 12 feet with minimal pruning.

BIG BLOOMS

Lavender star flower (*Grewia occidentalis*)

'Long John' grevillea (*Grevillea* 'Long John'): open lacy texture and coral flowers

'Moonlight' grevillea (*Grevillea* 'Moonlight'): large white exotic blooms that attract hummingbirds

'Slim' bottlebrush (*Callistemon viminalis* 'Slim'): red pom-pom blooms that bees love

Texas sage (*Leucophyllum frutescens*): silver foliage and purple blooms

EDIBLE HEDGES

Bay laurel (*Laurus nobilis*)

Blackberry (*Rubus fruticosus*)

Citrus (*Citrus*): our other favorite for hedges, using dwarf or standard citrus trees depending on the space

Pineapple guava (*Feijoa sellowiana*): silver foliage and edible blooms and fruit; our favorite edible hedge

Pomegranate (*Punica granatum*): fall color, fruit, and easy pruning

Can't-Live-Without Evergreen Shrubs

Asparagus densiflorus 'Myers'

Boxwood (*Buxus* 'Green Mountain'): deep green

Dwarf pittosporum (*Pittosporum crassifolium* 'Compactum'): light green

Dwarf variegated coast rosemary (*Westringia fruticosa* 'Grey Box'): gray

Dwarf yeddo hawthorn (*Rhaphiolepis umbellata* 'Minor'): deep green and rust

Little Ollie (*Olea europaea* 'Montra'): gray-green

Little river wattle (*Acacia cognata* 'Cousin Itt'): medium green

Smokey coast rosemary (*Westringia fruticosa* 'Smokey'): silver

Upright rosemary (*Romarinus* 'Tuscan Blue')

Variegated mirror plant (*Coprosma repens* 'Marble Queen')

White-margined euonymus (*Euonymous fortunei* 'Emerald Gaiety')

Medium Flowering Perennials

'Blue Spire' Russian sage (*Perovskia atriplicifolia* 'Blue Spire'): blue

Bruce's dwarf euphorbia (*Euphorbia characias* 'Bruce's Dwarf'): lime green

Chiapas sage (*Salvia chiapensis*): magenta

Fern-leaf yarrow (*Achillea filipendulina*): salmon to pink to yellow

Germander sage (*Salvia chamaedryoides*): indigo blue

Gray-leaved French lavender (*Lavandula dentata* var. *candicans*): lavender

Island alum root (*Heuchera maxima*): white

Japanese anemone (*Anemone* × hybrida 'Honorine Jobert'): white

Jerusalem sage (*Phlomis* 'Grande Verde'): gold

Kangaroo paw (*Anigozanthos* 'Big Red' and *A.* 'Harmony'): red, yellow, orange

Mexican Sage (*Salvia leucantha* 'Santa Barbara'): purple

Rozanne geranium (*Geranium* Rozanne = 'Gerwat'): purple

'Santa Ana Cardinal' coral bells (*Heuchera* 'Santa Ana Cardinal'): pink

Tall verbena (*Verbena bonariensis*): deep purple

'Waverly' sage (*Salvia* 'Waverly'): white and burgundy

Grasses

Autumn moor-grass (*Sesleria autumnalis*): medium upright, green clumping leaves with golden flower spikes

Berkeley sedge (*Carex tumulicola*): low, dark green arching leaves

Blue flax lily (*Dianella caerulea* 'Cassa Blue'): medium upright, blue clumping grasslike leaves with indigo flower spikes

Blue moor-grass (*Sesleria caerulea*): low, clumping grass with leaves that are green on top and silver blue on the underside

'Canyon Prince' wild rye (*Leymus condensatus* 'Canyon Prince'): medium, thick silver blue spreading with arching habit and tall golden flower spikes

Dwarf mat rush (*Lomandra longifolia* 'Breeze'): medium, arching delicate grasslike leaves with yellow flower spikes

Dwarf mondo grass (*Ophiopogon japonicus* 'Nana'): low, deep green clumping leaves

'Elijah Blue' blue fescue (*Festuca glauca* 'Elijah Blue'): low, delicate silver clumping leaves

Hare's tail (*Lagurus ovatus*): medium green grass with white flower tufts

'Karl Foerster' feather reed grass (*Calama-grostis* × *acutiflora* 'Karl Foerster'): tall, coarse green leaves with extra tall golden flower spikes

Mexican feather grass (*Nassella tenuissima*): medium green to golden, graceful, spreading grass (check local invasive list before planting)

Oriental fountain grass (*Pennisetum orientale*): medium spreading grass with rose-colored flower spikes.

Small cape rush (*Elegia tectorum*): medium grasslike plant with deep green reedlike leaves.

Ground Covers

'Biokovo' cranesbill (*Geranium × cantabrigiense* 'Biokovo'): green leaves with pale pink flowers

Ground morning glory (*Convolvulus sabatius*): creeping green foliage with purple blooms

Blue star creeper (*Isotoma fluviatilis*): delicate green leaves with abundant blue flowers

Common thyme (*Thymus vulgaris*): semi-woody green herb with white blossoms

Woolly thyme (*Thymus praecox*): low, dense, delicate green-gray leaves with purple flowers

Dwarf wall germander (*Teucrium chamaedrys* 'Nanum'): upright, spreading green leaves with pale purple flower spikes

Elfin thyme (*Thymus serpyllum* 'Elfin'): dense mat of delicate green leaves

Little ears (*Falkia repens*): bright green small leaves with white flowers

Prostrate rosemary (*Rosmarinus officinalis* 'Lockwood de Forest'): lowest-growing form of rosemary with semiwoody stems, needlelike leaves, and pale blue flowers

Sea thrift (*Armeria maritima*): delicate clumps of green leaves with small pink flower poufs

Silver carpet (*Dymondia margaretae*): dense mat of silver leaves with small yellow flowers

'Silver Falls' dichondra (*Dichondra argentea* 'Silver Falls'): spreading silver leaves

Trailing blue rosemary (*Rosmarinus officinalis* 'Irene'): low-growing, semiarching stems with green leaves and deep periwinkle flowers

'Walker's Low' catmint (*Nepeta racemosa* 'Walker's Low'): herbaceous green leaves with abundant indigo purple flowers

Plant List by Form

BRANCHED AND OPEN

Chaste tree (*Vitex agnus-castus*)

Giant bird of paradise (*Strelitzia nicolai*)

'Limelight' hydrangea (*Hydrangea paniculata* 'Limelight')

UPRIGHT AND VINING

Madagascar jasmine (*Stephanotis floribunda*)

Pretty Pink mandevilla (*Mandevilla ×* 'Sunparaprero')

Purple clematis (*Clematis viticella*)

DELICATE AND SPREADING

Coral bells (*Heuchera* 'Blackberry Ice')

Creeping Jenny (*Lysimachia nummularia*)

White bacopa (*Sutera cordata* 'Abunda Giant White')

ROSETTE AND ROUND

Echeveria spp

Giant leopard plant (*Farfugium gigantea*)

Rose blossoms (*Rosa* spp)

BUSHY AND FULL

'Green Beauty' boxwood (*Buxus microphylla* var. *japonica* 'Green Beauty')

Little Ollie (*Olea europaea* 'montra')

Little river wattle (*Acacia cognata* 'Cousin Itt')

FOUNTAIN AND ARCHING

Maiden grass (*Miscanthus sinensis* 'Gracillimus')

Rainbow New Zealand flax (*Phormium* 'Maori Maiden')

Variegated flax lily (*Dianella tasmanica* 'Variegata')

TRUNKED AND SCULPTURAL

Bay laurel (*Laurus nobilis*)

Dragon tree (*Dracaena marginata*)

Frangipani (*Plumeria*)

(See Best Box-Tree Bets, page 59)

CASCADING AND SPILLING

Petite licorice (*Helichrysum petiolare* 'Petite')

'Silver Falls' dichondra (*Dichondra argentea* 'Silver Falls'

Sweet potato vine (*Ipomoea batatas*)

Thank Yous!

A big thanks to our husbands, Darryl Eaton and Zack Kramer, who kept our homes running inside while we ran around outside, prepping and shooting in the gardens well before sunrise and long after sunset. Not only were they our number-one supporters from the get-go, but they were our ongoing photo-shoot light hangers, leaf blowers, plant preppers, pot movers, and bartenders. We love you and are so grateful as you really do make our souls blossom!

Thank you to our moms, Cassie Jane Hendry and Janis Blaise, who helped in the garden from planting lavender to lending their very own containers just when we needed them! And thanks to the kiddos (all of you!)—Samuel, Otis, Story, Stella, Julia, and Eloise—for your enthusiasm, your willingness to jump in (and your patience to jump out quietly!) while we made this book. To Teddy the miniature poodle, Lucy the black lab, and Hopper the neighborhood cat, you made such great stand-ins.

A huge thank you to our wildly creative photographer, Leela Cyd. We gained not just a talented eye throughout the project, but a lifelong friend.

To our agent, Lindsay Edgecombe, none of this would have been possible without you. Thank you for being our wise sounding board and friendly champion while finding this book a home.

Thank you to Ten Speed Press, including our editor, Lisa Regul, who was encouraging from the beginning and whose edits were always spot on, reminding us to stay small, yet think big; our creative director, Emma Campion, who was nearby for everything from on-set advice to the magical book-making process; and to Kim Keller and Dan Myers.

Merci to Anika Streitfeld for being our editorial compass as we stepped foot into the book world and to Marion Brenner and Siouxie Jennette for your early encouragement.

Thank you to Billy Dole and 7 Day Nursery for all your support for Isa Bird Gardens and for photo shoot details. Everyone should be so lucky to have a neighborhood nursery like you!

To all the wonderful friends and clients who opened up their homes and Isa Bird gardens to make this happen. Thank you, thank you Carolyn Bernstein and Nick Grad, Theresa Chase, Jill and Sam Ellis, Rachel Gaby, Heather Greene, Andrea Ridgell, Susan and Pat Schechter, Jessica Risko Smith, and Shelley and Kenny Van Zant. And to our models: Michelle Beamer; Dana Costello; Rita Donahoe; Darryl and Samuel Eaton; Mary Firestone; Andrew and Carolyn Fitzgerald; Cassie Keister; Eloise and Zack Kramer; Carrie Reilly; Nathan, Kaden, and Kashton Ridgell; and Becky Wilberding.

A special shout out to the help and talent from everyone who helped behind the scenes!

"Let us be grateful to the people who make us happy; they are the charming gardeners who make our souls blossom."

—Marcel Proust

Contributors

Nurseries

7 Day Nursery

Abe Nursery

Brightview

Giovannis Nursery

Monrovia

Norman's Nursery

Pianta Bella Nursery

San Marcos Growers

Terra Sol

Tony Krock

Gardeners and Landscape Contractors

Allscape Design + Installation

Arroyo Seco Constuction

Pacific Green Landscape Construction

Progressive Landscaping

Designers and Architects

Becker Studios

Dan Weber Architects

Jessica Risko Smith

Makeshift Studio

Talia Jones Roston

Food Styling

Becky Sue Wilberding, Baking the Goods

Accessories

Anthropologie

Campania International

CB2

Design Within Reach

Diani Living

Fermob

Innit Designs

Pioneer Synthetic Turf

Pottery Barn

Restoration Hardware

Riviera Towel

Teak Warehouse

Tractor Supply Company

Urban Outfitters

West Elm

World Market

"Style translates from our closet to our living room to our garden."

Index

A

Acacia cognata 'Cousin Itt', 114, 136, 176, 177
A. podalyriifolia, 18, 174
Acer palmatum, 59, 174
Achillea filipendulina, 114, 176
Acorus gramineus 'Minimus Aureus', 43
Actinidia arguta, 110, 175
A. canariense, 18, 40, 43, 136
A. haworthii 'Kiwi', 122
Agave americana, 40, 50, 124
A. attenuata, 50, 70
A. celsii 'Nova', 68
A. desmettiana 'Variegata', 70
A. potatorum 'El Camaron', 40, 128
Akebia quinata, 175
Aloe 'Rooikappie', 70
A. striata, 124
  × *maculata*, 78
Anemone × *hybrida* 'Honorine Jobert', 176
Anigozanthos, 50, 176
annuals, 107, 172
Arabian lilac. See *Vitex trifolia* 'Purpurea'
Arbutus 'Marina', 50, 174
Archontophoenix cunninghamiana, 77
Armeria maritima, 121, 177
artificial turf, 88, 90
Asparagus densiflorus 'Myers' (asparagus fern), 27, 43, 139, 176
Asplenium nidus, 136
asymmetrical layouts, 66
Australian violet. See *Viola hederacea*
autumn moor-grass. See *Sesleria autumnalis*
awnings, 101
azalea, 98, 175

B

balance, 66
Bambusa oldhamii, 30
bay laurel. See *Laurus nobilis*
Beaucarnea recurvata, 46
bees, 120
Berkeley sedge. See *Carex divulsa; C. tumulicola*
blackberry. See *Rubus fruticosus*
blue Atlas cedar. See *Cedrus atlantica* 'Glauca Pendula'
blue fan palm. See *Brahea armata*
blue moor-grass. See *Sesleria caerulea*
blue star creeper. See *Isotoma fluviatilis*
Bold Eclectic style, 24, 26–27, 84–85

Boston ivy. See *Parthenocissus tricuspidata* 'Veitchii'
Bougainvillea, 54, 174
boulders, 93
box trees, 56, 59
boxwood. See *Buxus*
Brahea armata, 44, 46, 174
brick, 90
Buchloe dactyloides, 88
buffalo grass. See *Buchloe dactyloides*
butterflies, 120
Buxus, 114, 139, 176, 177

C

Calamagrostis × *acutiflora* 'Karl Foerster', 117, 176
Calliandra haematocephala, 98, 175
Callistemon viminalis 'Slim', 84, 85, 175
camellia, 175
Canary Island date palm. See *Phoenix canariensis*
Carex divulsa, 30, 117
C. flacca 'Blue Zinger', 124
C. tumulicola, 176
Cassia leptophylla, 174
Cedrus atlantica 'Glauca Pendula', 174
century plant. See *Agave americana*
Cercis canadensis 'Forest Pansy', 108, 174
C. occidentalis, 108, 174
Ceropegia woodii, 27
chaste tree. See *Vitex agnus-castus*
Chiapas sage. See *Salvia chiapensis*
Chinese money plant. See *Pilea peperomioides*
chocolate vine. See *Akebia quinata*
Chondropetalum tectorum, 18
Cistanthe grandiflora 'Jazz Time', 37
citrus
  container gardens, 144
  trees, 113, 175
Citrus × *limon*, 54, 175
Clean Minimalist style, 40, 43
clematis, 174, 177
color, 37, 70, 73
Color Play style, 50, 53
container gardens
  advantages of, 1, 127
  building, step by step, 131–39
  caring for, 156
  citrus, 144
  as focal points, 68, 128, 154
  at front door, 154

as garden walls, 94, 95, 98
  location for, 131
  picking plants for, 139, 141, 143, 156
  scale and size of, 132
  single, 136
  styles and materials for, 134–35, 139, 148
  succulents in, 122
  tabletop, 152–53
  trio of, 136
  uses for, 128, 131
  veggie, 146, 148
Continus coggygria, 174
contrast, 82–83
Convolvulus sabatius, 54, 121, 177
Cool Restaurant style, 26–27
coppertone stonecrop. See *Sedum nussbaumerianum*
Coprosma repens 'Marble Queen', 30, 176
Cordyline australis 'Torbay Dazzler', 85
Cornus kousa 'Miss Satomi', 174
Cotinus coggygria, 174
Cotyledon orbiculata, 18
crape myrtle. See *Lagerstroemia indica*
creeping fig. See *Ficus pumila*
creeping Jenny. See *Lysimachia nummularia*
cup of gold vine. See *Solandra maxima*
Cupressus sempervirens 'Monshel', 54
curved layouts, 66

D

daybeds, 53
deadheading, 172
deciduous, definition of, 172
decks, 40, 89, 90, 162, 172
Delosperma nubigenum, 85
design principles
  #1. Line + Space, 66–67
  #2. Focal Point, 68
  #3. Eye Candy, 70, 72–74, 76–77
  #4. Layering + Repetition, 78
  #5. Contrast, 82–83
Dianella caerulea 'Cassa Blue', 117, 176
D. tasmanica 'Variegata', 177
Dichondra argentea 'Silver Falls', 43, 54, 119, 121, 177
Diospyros kaki 'Fuyu', 174
Distictis laxiflora 'Vanilla Orchid', 110, 175
D. 'Rivers', 110, 175
DIY vs. hiring out, 167
donkey's tail. See *Sedum morganianum*

Dracaena draco, 44
D. marginata, 44, 177
drainage
for container gardens, 156
definition of, 172
permeable floors for, 88
drought-tolerant, definition of, 172
dwarf golden sweet flag. *See
Acorus gramineus* 'Minimus
Aureus'
dwarf mat rush. *See Lomandra
longifolia* 'Breeze'
dwarf mondo grass. *See
Ophiopogon japonicus*
'Nana'
dwarf yeddo hawthorn. *See
Rhaphiolepis umbellata*
'Minor'
Dymondia margaretae, 37, 50,
70, 90, 119, 177

E
Echeveria
'Afterglow', 40, 85
'Black Prince', 153
'Cante', 18
'Joan Daniel', 122
'Perle Von Nürnberg', 70, 122, 145
E. agavoides
'Dark Prince', 122
'Ebony', 18
'Lipstick', 85
E. cante, 122
E. colorata, 122
E. elegans, 18, 70, 97, 122, 145
E. imbricata, 18, 39
E. lilacina, 143
E. minima, 153
E. grusonii, 40
egress view, 172
80/20 rule, 114
Elegia tectorum, 117, 143, 176
espalier, 98
Eucalyptus 'Moon Lagoon', 37
Euonymus fortunei 'Emerald
Gaiety', 176
Euphorbia characias 'Bruce's
Dwarf', 176
E. trigona, 44
evergreen, definition of, 172
eye candy, 70, 72–74, 76–77

F
Falkia repens, 119, 177
The Fantastic Five, 63, 65, 84.
See also design principles
Farfugium gigantea, 177
Feijoa sellowiana, 113, 175
fern-leaf yarrow. *See Achillea
filipendulina*
fern pine. *See Podocarpus
gracilior*

fertilizers, 156, 169
Festuca glauca 'Elijah Blue', 18,
50, 117, 176
Ficus carica, 59, 174
F. elastica, 27, 44, 46
F. pumila, 110, 175
F. triangularis, 24
fire pits, 18, 20, 22, 68
flags, landscape, 164, 166
flagstone, 90
flame vine. *See Pyrostegia
venusta*
flowers
edible, 113, 146, 148, 150
foliage vs., 107
perennial, 114, 176
focal points
containers for, 68, 128, 154
definition of, 172
as design principle, 68
trees as, 50, 109
types of, 68
form, 74, 139, 141, 177
Fortunella margarita 'Nagami', 145
frangipani. *See Plumeria*
front door, container garden
at, 154

G
garden rooms
ceilings for, 101
concept of, 5, 87
floors for, 88–90, 93, 97
walls for, 94–95, 97–98
gardens
assessing space for, 160
elevator pitch for, 8
identifying function of, 9
maintaining, 169
planning, 162–66
See also container gardens;
design principles; garden
rooms; style
Geranium × cantabrigiense
'Biokovo', 68, 177
G. 'Gerwat', 124, 176
germander sage. *See Salvia
chamaedryoides*
giant bird of paradise. *See
Strelitzia nicolai*
giant leopard plant. *See
Farfugium gigantea*
Global Boho style, 44, 46
golden Japanese forest grass.
See Hakonechloa macra
'Aureola'
gold medallion tree. *See Cassia
leptophylla*
grape vine. *See Vitis vinifera*
Graptopetalum amethystinum, 153
G. paraguayense, 18, 50, 122, 143

Graptosedum 'Darley
Sunshine', 85
Graptoveria 'Fred Ives', 122
grasses
alternative, 88, 90
fake, 88, 90
for lawns, 88
ornamental, 116–17
recommended, 176
gravel, 88, 90
Grevillea, 113, 175
Grewia occidentalis, 70, 98, 175
grid layouts, 66
ground covers
definition of, 118, 172
examples of, 119, 121
for pollinators, 120
recommended, 176–77

H
Hakonechloa macra 'Aureola', 43
Hardenbergia violacea
'Canoelands', 175
hardscape
definition of, 172
planning, 162, 163–64
texture of, 76–77
hardy kiwi. *See Actinidia arguta*
hare's tail. *See Lagurus ovatus*
Hedera helix, 30
hedges
containers for, 128
edible, 113, 175
as garden walls, 94
recommended, 113
Helichrysum petiolare
'Petite', 177
hens and chicks. *See
Sempervivum* 'Blue Boy'
Heuchera
'Blackberry Ice', 177
'Santa Ana Cardinal', 176
H. maxima, 176
high-to-low plant selection,
105–6, 124
hiring out vs. DIY, 167
Howea forsteriana, 24
Hoya carnosa, 27, 136
hummingbirds, 120
Humulus lupulus, 175
Hydrangea paniculata
'Limelight', 37, 177

I
Instant Orchard, 56
Ipomoea batatas, 177
I. indica, 124
irrigation, 169
island alum root. *See Heuchera
maxima*
Isotoma fluviatilis, 121, 177

J

Jacaranda mimosifolia, 124
Japanese maple. See Acer palmatum
Japanese persimmon. See Diospyros kaki 'Fuyu'
Jerusalem sage. See Phlomis 'Grande Verde'

K

kangaroo paw. See Anigozanthos
king palm. See Archontophoenix cunninghamiana

L

Lagerstroemia indica, 59, 108, 174
Lagurus ovatus, 117, 176
Larix decidua pendula, 174
Laurus nobilis, 59, 175, 177
Lavandula dentata var. candicans, 114, 176
L. stoechas 'Otto Quast', 54
lavender star flower. See Grewia occidentalis
lawns, 88
layering, 78
Leucadendron 'Winter Red', 18
Leucophyllum frutescens, 175
Leymus condensatus 'Canyon Prince', 37, 50, 117, 176
lighting, 24, 54
Ligustrum, 59
L. japonica 'Texanum', 113, 114, 124, 128, 175
line and space, 66–67
Lippia nodiflora 'Kurapia', 77, 90
little ears. See Falkia repens
little river wattle. See Acacia cognata 'Cousin Itt'
Lomandra longifolia 'Breeze', 117, 124, 176
Lonicera hildebrandiana, 175
loungers, 53
Lysimachia nummularia, 139, 177

M

Madagascar jasmine. See Stephanotis floribunda
Magnolia grandiflora 'Little Gem', 59, 108, 174
maiden grass. See Miscanthus sinensis 'Gracillimus'
maintenance, 169
Mandevilla × 'Sunparaprero', 177
Maranta leuconeura, 24
Maytenus boaria, 174
Mexican feather grass. See Nassella tenuissima
Mexican gem. See Echeveria elegans
Mexican sage. See Salvia leucantha 'Santa Barbara'

Miscanthus sinensis 'Gracillimus', 177
morning glory. See Ipomoea indica
mother-in-law's tongue. See Sansevieria trifasciata
mother-of-pearl plant. See Graptopetalum paraguayense
mulch, 90, 172
Myoporum 'Putah Creek', 90

N

Nassella tenuissima, 50, 117, 128, 176
negative space, 66
Neoregelia carolinae, 44
Nepeta racemosa 'Walker's Low', 37, 121, 177
New Traditional style, 34, 37

O

Old World style, 54, 56, 59
Olea europaea (olive)
    'Montra', 30, 54, 74, 94, 114, 139, 176, 177
    'Swan Hill', 85, 174
    'Wilsonii', 50, 59, 108
Ophiopogon japonicus 'Nana', 97, 117, 176
Organic Modern style, 18, 20
Oriental fountain grass. See Pennisetum orientale
Origanum vulgare, 30
Oscularia deltoides, 85, 122, 145

P

Pachycereus marginatus, 40
Parkinsonia aculeata (palo verde), 59
P. 'Desert Museum', 109, 174
Parthenocissus tricuspidata 'Veitchii', 110, 175
parties, 56
pathways, 88, 163–64, 172
patios, 24, 88, 172
pavers, 40, 67, 90
pearl acacia. See Acacia podalyriifolia
Pennisetum orientale, 117, 176
Peperomia obtusifolia, 44
perennials
    definition of, 172
    recommended, 176
pergolas, 101
Perovskia atriplicifolia 'Blue Spire', 114, 176
Phlomis 'Grande Verde', 114, 176
Phoenix canariensis, 77
Phormium, 50, 177
Pilea peperomioides, 27
pineapple guava. See Feijoa sellowiana
pink iceplant. See Oscularia deltoides

pink powder puff tree. See Calliandra haematocephala
Pistia stratiotes, 46
Pittosporum crassifolium 'Compactum', 54, 114, 176
plants
    for container gardens, 139, 141, 143, 156
    flagging, 166
    forms of, 74, 139, 141, 177
    high-to-low design for, 105–6
    layout for, 165–66
    recommended, 174–77
    scientific names for, 172
    selection pitfalls for, 107
    texture of, 77
    See also individual plants
Plumeria, 40, 43, 174, 177
P. gracilior, 113, 175
pollinators, ground covers for, 120
Polystichum munitum, 24
pomegranate. See Punica granatum
ponytail palm. See Beaucarnea recurvata
pork and beans. See Sedum rubrotinctum
positive space, 66
"Power Couple" system, 143
privet. See Ligustrum
proportion, 66
pruning
    deadheading, 172
    tip, 170
Prunus caroliniana 'Monus', 175
Punica granatum, 174, 175
pups, 172
purple lilac vine. See Hardenbergia violacea 'Canoelands'
Pyrostegia venusta, 110, 175
Pyrus calleryana 'Jaczam', 174

Q

queen palm. See Syagrus romanzoffiana
Quercus agrifolia, 18

R

repetition, 78
Rhaphiolepis umbellata 'Minor', 114, 176
Rhipsalis baccifera, 24, 139
Rhododendron, 98, 175
Rosa
    'Cècile Brünnerr', 174
    'Eden', 174
    'Iceberg', 37, 124
    'Sally Holmes', 175
Rosmarinus officinalis, 37, 121, 176, 177
royal trumpet vine. See Distictis 'Rivers'
Rubus fruticosus, 175

S

Salvia chamaedryoides, 85, 176
S. chiapensis, 124, 176
S. leucantha 'Santa Barbara', 114, 176
Sansevieria trifasciata, 46
scale, 30, 66, 132
scientific plant names, 172
screening plants, 113, 175
seasonality, 172
sea thrift. *See Armeria maritima*
Sedeveria 'Green Rose', 122
Sedum clavatum, 68
S. × cremnosedum 'Little Gem', 122
S. morganianum, 74, 122, 139
S. nussbaumerianum, 50, 85, 122
S. rowleyanus, 143
S. rubrotinctum, 122
S. rupestre, 122
Sempervivum 'Blue Boy', 122
S. calcareum, 122
S. tectorum, 122
Senecio cylindricustalinoides subsp. *cylindricus*, 70
S. mandraliscae, 50, 78
S. radicans, 24, 68, 74
S. rowleyanus, 122
S. rupestre, 70, 122, 143
S. serpens, 70, 122
S. talinoides subsp. *cylindricus*, 122
Sesleria autumnalis, 18, 50, 117, 176
S. caerulea, 18, 85, 117, 176
setback, 172
shade sails, 101
shape vs. form, 74
shower, outdoor, 43
shrubs
    deciduous, 172
    definition of, 172
    evergreen, 114, 176
    tall, 113, 175
silver carpet. *See Dymondia margaretae*
small cape rush. *See Elegia tectorum*
smoke tree. *See Cotinus coggygria*
soil
    amending, 169
    for container gardens, 156
    testing, 169
Solandra maxima, 110, 174
space
    line and, 66–67
    negative, 66
    positive, 66
    scale and, 30
Stachys byzantina 'Helen von Stein', 82, 124

star jasmine. *See Trachelospermum jasminoides*
Stephanotis floribunda, 27, 37, 177
strawberry tree. *See Arbutus* 'Marina'
Strelitzia nicolai, 177
string of beads. *See Senecio rowleyanus*
string of fishhooks. *See Senecio radicans*
string of hearts. *See Ceropegia woodii*
style
    Bold Eclectic, 24, 26–27, 84–85
    Clean Minimalist, 40, 43
    Color Play, 50, 53
    for container gardens, 134–35, 139, 148
    Cool Restaurant, 26–27
    finding personal, 7, 10, 12, 14–15
    Global Boho, 44, 46
    mood and, 10
    New Traditional, 34, 37
    Old World, 54, 56, 59
    Organic Modern, 18, 20
    quiz, 12, 14–15
    Urban Homestead, 30, 33
succulents, 30, 70, 122
Sutera cordata 'Abunda Giant White', 177
sweet potato vine. *See Ipomoea batatas*
Syagrus romanzoffiana, 77
symmetrical layouts, 66

T

tabletop container arrangements, 152–53
Teucrium ackermannii, 54
T. chamaedrys, 30, 121, 177
Texas privet. *See Ligustrum japonica* 'Texanum'
Texas sage. *See Leucophyllum frutescens*
texture, 44, 76–77
Thrill, Fill, and Spill rule, 143
Thymus praecox, 119, 177
T. serpyllum, 85, 119, 121, 177
T. vulgaris, 30, 121, 177
Tillandsia usneoides, 44
tip pruning, 170
Trachelospermum jasminoides, 98, 175
trees
    box, 56, 59
    choosing, 109
    deciduous, 172
    espalier, 98, 175
    evergreen, 172
    as focal points, 50, 68, 109
    as garden ceilings, 101

Instant Orchard, 56
    number of types of, 107, 109
    recommended, 108, 174
    working with, 109
trellises, 98, 101

U

umbrellas, 101
underplant, definition of, 172
Urban Homestead style, 30, 33

V

vanilla trumpet vine. *See Distictis laxiflora* 'Vanilla Orchid'
veggie container gardens, 146, 148
Verbena bonariensis, 114, 176
vines
    choosing, 110
    espalier, 98, 175
    patterned, 98, 175
    recommended, 110, 174–75
Viola hederacea, 119
Vitex agnus-castus, 177
V. trifolia 'Purpurea', 108, 174
Vitis vinifera, 175

W

water features
    boulders for, 93
    definition of, 172
    fire and, 46
    as focal points, 68
watering, 156, 169
water lettuce. *See Pistia stratiotes*
wax plant. *See Hoya carnosa*
western redbud. *See Cercis occidentalis*
Westringia fruticosa, 37, 114, 176
white, use of, 83
wisteria, 110, 174
woolly thyme. *See Thymus praecox*
wreaths, 34, 39

Z

Zamioculcas zamiifolia, 44

Library of Congress Cataloging-in-Publication Data
Names: Eaton, Isa Hendry, 1976– author. |
Kramer, Jennifer Blaise, 1978– author.
Title: Small garden style : a design guide for outdoor rooms and containers /
Isa Hendry Eaton and Jennifer Blaise Kramer ; photography by Leela Cyd.
Description: First edition. | Oakland [Calif.] : Ten Speed Press, 2020. |
Includes index.
Identifiers: LCCN 2019014809 | ISBN 9780399582851 (hardcover)
Subjects: LCSH: Container gardening. | Small gardens.
Classification: LCC SB418 .E32 2020 | DDC 635.9/86—dc23 LC record
available at https://lccn.loc.gov/2019014809

Hardcover ISBN: 978-0-399-58285-1
eBook ISBN: 978-0-399-58286-8

Printed in China

Design by Emma Campion

10 9 8 7 6 5 4 3 2

First Edition